GRACE HOPPER

Navy Admiral and Computer Pioneer

Charlene W. Billings

ENSLOW PUBLISHERS, INC.

Bloy St. & Ramsey Ave.	P.O. Box 38
Box 777	Aldershot
Hillside, N.J. 07205	Hants GU12 6BP
U.S.A.	U.K.

Library of Congress Cataloging-in-Publication Data

Billings, Charlene W.
    Grace Hopper: navy admiral and computer pioneer / by Charlene W. Billings.
        p. cm.
    Includes index.
    Summary: Traces the life of the scientist who, as well as having a distinguished career in the Navy, was a pioneer contributor to computer science and is known as the grandmother of the computer age.
        ISBN 0-89490-194-X
        1. Hopper, Grace Murray—Juvenile literature. 2. Admirals—United States—Biography—Juvenile literature. 3. Computer engineers—United States—Biography—Juvenile literature. 4. United States. Navy—Women—Biography—Juvenile literature. [1. Hopper, Grace Murray. 2. Admirals. 3. Computer engineers. 4. United States. Navy—Women—Biography.] I. Title.
V63.H66B55   1989
359'.0092—dc20
[B]   89-1523
                                          CIP
                                          AC

Printed in the United States of America

10 9 8 7 6 5 4 3 2

Courtesy, Vassar College Library:
Quotation of C. Mildred Thompson, as reported in "Academic Year Begins," in *The Miscellany News*, 27 September 1924: pp. 23-24.

Illustrations Courtesy of:
Brewster Academy Archives: p. 107; Cruft Photo Lab, Harvard University, Photo by Paul Donaldson: pp. 45, 48; Grace Murray Hopper: p. 14; International Business Machines Corp.: pp. 42, 54, 62; National Archives: pp. 35; National Oceanic and Atmospheric Administration, National Weather Service: p. 100; UNISYS: pp. 69, 75, 83, 84, 89; U.S. Navy Photo: pp. 11, 59, 95 (by PH2 David C. MacLean), 105 (by Bill Mason), 109 (by Pete Souza), 110; Vassar College Library: pp. 25, 27; Vassar Press and Information Office, Dixie Sheridan: p. 26; Mary Murray Wescote: pp. 19, 21, 31, 112.

Cover photo: Official U.S. Navy Photo

To Grace Murray Hopper,
who believes in young people everywhere

Acknowledgments

I wish to thank the many helpful people who provided information and photographs for this book. Dr. Grace Murray Hopper generously gave her time to answer questions about her childhood, family, student days, and career during several telephone calls and later in person in Washington, D.C. She ended each of our conversations with an offer to be of further assistance. Dr. Hopper also sent reprints of articles she wrote, information about the development of computer languages, and photographs.

Dr. and Mrs. Roger F. Murray II invited me to their summer cottage on Lake Wentworth in Wolfeboro, New Hampshire, where Dr. Murray reminisced about his family and growing up with his sisters.

Mrs. Mary Murray Westcote responded to my request for help to write a biography about her sister with an enjoyable and informative telephone call and also sent copies of family photographs.

In addition, two of Dr. Hopper's former students, Dr. Winifred Asprey and Dr. Anne O'Neill, enthusiastically talked with me about Grace Hopper and how she influenced them to become mathematicians and teachers.

At Brewster Academy, Judy Valade made available a large file of information that the school maintains about Dr. Hopper, and she and Jason Thatcher took me to visit the Grace Murray Hopper Center for Computer Learning. Brewster Academy also allowed me to use many of their photographs.

Alice F. Vorwerk, Director of Admissions at the Wardlaw-

Hartridge School, and Nancy S. Burleson searched for and sent information about the school as it was during Grace Hopper's student days.

Nancy S. MacKechnie, Curator of Rare Books and Manuscripts, and other staff members at Vassar College cooperated to provide photographs and materials for this biography.

Thank you to Dr. Gwen Bell and to Lynn Hall of the Computer Museum, Boston, Massachusetts, for talking with me and for sending information about Dr. Hopper, Dr. Howard Aiken, and computers.

In addition, my appreciation to my neighbor, Lena Robert, who is employed by Digital Equipment Corporation, for bringing me articles and video tapes about Grace Hopper's colorful life and career. Also, thanks to her husband, Dennis, for assisting me to make copies of the tapes.

Finally, thank you to the personnel of the United States Navy who helped to locate photographs and information and especially to Lieutenant Commander Brenda Sullivan for providing an extensive bibliography she had prepared about Dr. Hopper.

—C.W.B.

Contents

1

A Fond Farewell

With great joy, 275 dignitaries, family members, friends, Navy officials, and crew gathered on "Old Ironsides" to honor retiring Rear Admiral Grace Murray Hopper. The date was August 14, 1986. At age seventy-nine, Admiral Hopper was the oldest commissioned officer on active duty in the United States Navy, and her final request had been granted. She wanted her retirement ceremony conducted aboard the U.S.S. *Constitution*, the nation's oldest commissioned warship, saying, "I love this ship. We belong together."

As she sat under sunny skies near the great ship's shiny brass bell, surrounded by the colorful rigging of the top deck and thirty-two pound carronades, Rear Admiral Hopper may have wished that the hands on the backward clock in her office could have been stopped the day before at one minute to midnight. Then the date of her retirement from the United States Navy would not have arrived. She had loved every day of duty in the Navy.

To those who had served with and under Admiral Hopper, she was respectfully and lovingly known as "Amazing Grace." Friends and admirers describe her as a tireless, vigorous, witty, and occasionally contrary woman who smokes unfiltered cigarettes and has a résumé several pages long of awards, honorary degrees and professional activities.

Grace Hopper has said, "Most people are scared to death of change and I am not. Some of my most rewarding experiences have been in trying to do something in a new way." To emphasize this philosophy, she keeps a clock in her office that runs counter-clockwise. The numbers on the face of the clock are backward too, so you can still tell time as easily as with an ordinary clock. But the backward clock reminds people that Admiral Hopper refuses to listen to the words, "But we've always done it that way!" She says that phrase is "the worst in the English language."

Newspaper reporters and other news personnel were on board ship to record the events of the grandest retirement ceremony ever held on the 188-year-old frigate at the Charlestown Naval Shipyard in Boston, Massachusetts.

With the ceremony under way, Secretary of the Navy John F. Lehman, Jr., spoke about Admiral Hopper. "She's challenged at every turn the dictates of mindless bureaucracy," he said. He also recalled that once Admiral Hopper "gave me a stern lecture on computers. It was the roughest wire brushing I've had since I got this job."

Then Secretary Lehman pinned onto Admiral Hopper's dress white uniform the Distinguished Service Medal of the Defense Department for exceptional meritorious service to the United States. This medal is the Defense Department's highest honor.

A portion of the accompanying citation presented to Admiral Hopper read: "Rear Admiral Hopper's personal dedication, technical expertise, and broad-based knowledge of the computers were a cornerstone of the Navy's continuing development of Information Systems technology. She is one of the Navy's most effective public speakers and a sought-after adviser on the subject of automatic data processing."

The citation also stated: "She gained international renown for her work in developing the COBOL programming language . . . Admiral Hopper not only championed the continuing evolution of information systems, but she is also a renowned ambassador for the Navy."

In her acceptance speech, Admiral Hopper paid special thanks to those who worked with her during World War II. Some of them were present to see her retire. She also praised the U.S.S. *Constitution* and the museum associated with the ship, the Boston Computer Museum, and the Constitution itself. She reminded everyone that America's historic document would celebrate its bicentennial the next year.

Commander Joseph Z. Brown of the U.S.S. *Constitution* presents Admiral Grace Hopper with forty-three long-stemmed roses during retirement ceremonies on August 14, 1986.

In addition to her award from the Defense Department, Admiral Hopper was named the First Fellow of the Boston Computer Museum. Dr. Gwen Bell, president and director of the Boston Computer Museum, presented a beaming Admiral Hopper with a large silicon chip tied to a ribbon.

While an eighteen-piece Navy band played patriotic songs, Commander Joseph Z. Brown—the sixty-first officer in command of the U.S.S. *Constitution* and clothed in a War of 1812 uniform— presented Admiral Hopper with forty-three long-stemmed roses—one for each year of her Navy career.

As she walked across the deck to leave the U.S.S. *Constitution* for a luncheon reception, seamen in traditional 1812 garb scampered up the warship's rigging and cheered in unison:

"HUZZAH!...HUZZAH!...HUZZAH!"

This was their special salute for the diminutive, white-haired woman who is regarded as the grandmother of the computer age. Grace Hopper helped to modernize the United States Navy by standardizing the way the Navy uses computers.

2

An Adventurous Childhood

Grace Brewster Murray was born in New York City on December 9, 1906. Approximately three years earlier, on December 17, 1903, Orville Wright had piloted the first successful flight of a power-driven airplane near Kitty Hawk, North Carolina. Henry Ford's famous Model T, the first automobile built with standardized parts and assembly-line techniques, would not roll off the production line until 1908. And not until eight years after Grace's birth would Alexander Graham Bell make the first transcontinental telephone call from New York to San Francisco. Mathematicians and engineers of the day used slide rules, devices that had existed as early as the 1700s, to do complicated calculations.

First child of Mary Campbell Van Horne Murray and Walter Fletcher Murray, Grace was warmly welcomed into the household. She was named after her mother's life-long best friend, Grace Brewster.

The Murrays and the Van Hornes had called New York City their home for several generations. Grace's father worked as an insurance broker for the firm of R. F. Murray and Brother. Walter Murray's father also had been an insurance man and had moved

Grace Brewster Murray clutching her doll and wishing that her long woolen stockings would stay up.

with his family from Scotland to New York City at the age of eleven. His father, in turn, had been a builder who helped construct a reservoir that used to be located behind the main building of the New York Public Library.

John Van Horne, Grace Murray's grandfather on her mother's side of the family, was a senior civil engineer for the City of New York. He laid out the streets in upper New York City and knew them like the palm of his hand.

As a young girl, Grace's mother sometimes would accompany her father on surveying trips in the city. She loved mathematics, and special arrangements were made so that she could study geometry seated by a window in the hallway at school. But she did not take algebra or trigonometry. In the late 1800s it was unthinkable for a young woman to undertake a serious study of mathematics. Later, young Grace would occasionally go surveying with her grandfather as well. She loved mathematics, too, and enjoyed holding the tall, red-and-white surveyor's range pole for him as he worked.

When Grace was about three years old, her sister Mary was born, and two years later her brother Roger joined the family.

While Grace, Mary, and Roger were children, their father developed serious hardening of the arteries in his legs. At that time, there was no medical treatment available. By the time Grace was in her first year of high school, both of her father's legs had been amputated.

After long hospitalizations Walter Murray returned to work, managing to get around on heavy wooden legs with the aid of two canes. He often would talk to other amputees, helping them to find the courage to go on with their lives.

He used to say to his children that if he could walk with two wooden legs and two canes, they could do anything. Grace Hopper has said her father was an excellent testimonial to the adage, "You can overcome things if you want to." For the Murray children, their father's handicap was an extra reason for achievement. When they went to school, they wanted to bring back A's for Dad.

Today, Grace recalls that her father believed his daughters should have the same educational opportunities as his son. He had lived through the Panic of 1893, a long, dismal economic period, and he had seen the daughters of some of his friends unable to get jobs because they did not have any training.

Grace says that her father encouraged her to leave behind the usual feminine roles of the time. He urged her and her brother and sister to go to college. And he wanted each of his daughters to work for at least one year after completing college to insure that they would be able to support themselves. He used to tell his children that he might not be able to leave them any money, but he could see to it that they were trained.

Walter Murray's questionable health made Grace's mother concerned that she might become a widow at any time. She learned to keep complete financial records for the family and to manage the family's finances. In this way, her interest in numbers and mathematics filled a practical need. As things turned out, Walter Murray lived to be seventy-five.

Keenly remembered in Grace's early childhood is an event that occurred when she was three years old. One night in May 1910, Grace recalls that her father held her up to the kitchen window to see Halley's Comet. It appeared to her as bigger and brighter than the full moon. She says that night, her father predicted she would live to see it return in 1986. He was right.

Memories of childhood activities for all of the Murray children are happy. Roger recalls that he had "a wonderful set of electric trains," as well as a kit of Structo metal building pieces. He still can quote the toy company's slogan, "Structo Toys make men of boys."

In addition, the three Murray children played with a set of stone blocks that came in many sizes and shapes. They were imported from Germany and included blueprint-like plans that the children carefully followed to make a church with a steeple or other buildings.

A set of peg-lock blocks came in sizes that were variations on two inches, such as two by two or two by four. The blocks in this set had openings in the edges so that they could be locked together. Grace loved building things with this set because the blocks could not be knocked over easily.

A Structiron construction kit of nuts, bolts, and other metal pieces was one of Grace's favorite toys. The set included a small electrical motor so you could build elevators and pull things.

Reading was Grace's favorite pastime. She says books always were tops on her Christmas wish list. She remembers a series that was passed on to her by her mother in which a little girl took part in the founding of each of the great cities of the United States. Other series told stories collected from all the nations or related the big events of world history. Grace was enchanted by the "marvelous rhythm" of Rudyard Kipling's *Just So Stories* and can freely recite lines from them now. She also enjoyed *St. Nicholas* magazine and recalls that she first read Frances Burnett's *The Secret Garden* in that publication.

Grace had a marvelous dollhouse with tiny figures that she still keeps today. However, she did not have her dollhouse family do things. Instead, she made furniture, curtains, and rugs for them. She also made clothes for them as well as for her and her sister's larger dolls.

Early in her life Grace learned to knit, crochet, and do needlework. She remembers her first knitting project, which she undertook when she was very young. It was a washcloth for her father. She says, "It was about ten inches across at the top and about sixteen inches on the bottom. My father admired it and thanked me for it."

Grace took piano lessons and played the instrument until she was in her thirties. She and her brother and sister also enjoyed singing together around the piano as their mother played.

Some of Grace's happiest times were the summers spent at the family's cottage in the Point Breeze area on Lake Wentworth in Wolfeboro, New Hampshire. Her grandfather had originally bought the property because of the great bass fishing the area provided.

One day in Wolfeboro, when she was seven years old, Grace could not stem her curiosity and decided that she had to find out how her alarm clock worked. (She says even now that she cannot resist a good gadget!) The cottage at Lake Wentworth had seven bedrooms to accommodate her many cousins who came during the summer to visit. And each bedroom had an alarm clock—the kind with a round face, two feet, and a big bell on top.

First Grace took the clock in her bedroom apart but could not figure out how to put it back together. So she took the clock in the next bedroom apart. Still she had no luck reassembling the pieces. And thus she continued through the bedrooms, eventually undoing all seven clocks. After her mother found out what had happened, Grace was restricted to one clock.

As the oldest of three children, Grace says that she always took "the brunt of everything." For example, one summer day at Lake Wentworth, she and a bunch of cousins were caught climbing in a pine tree. Since she was at the top, she says that it was obvious who started it. She lost her swimming privileges for a week.

Grace says that she, Roger, Mary, and their many cousins in Wolfeboro played games like kick-the-can, hide-and-seek, and cops-and-robbers. She adds that she and the other kids took their kick-the-can games very seriously.

In addition to the other summer activities, the Murray children had to learn to do certain things when they were in Wolfeboro. Grace and Mary both learned to do needlepoint and cross-stitch and even Roger had to learn how to sew on a button. Their mother

Grace Murray (on the left) as a child with her father, sister, and infant brother at the family cottage on Lake Wentworth, Wolfeboro, New Hampshire.

insisted that all of them learn to plant and grow things in the garden and to cook as well.

An adventure Grace tells about happened when she had a sail-canoe. While her mother watched, Grace says, "I sailed down the lake one day tacked into the wind. And then I turned around to fly before the wind coming back. And the wind freshened—got *very* strong. And the big waves broke over the stern of the canoe and it was getting full of water . . . . By the time I got opposite the front porch, she [the canoe] was way down in the water, particularly in the stern where I was. Mother got the megaphone that she used to call us off the lake and yelled at me, 'Don't go down by the stern. What would your great-grandfather [who had been a Rear Admiral in the Navy] say?' So I tipped her over and towed her into shore. I did not go down by the stern."

In the winter months there was school. Grace attended the Graham School, as had her mother before her, and Schoonmakers School in New York City. Early education in private schools was considered normal in those days. The schools for girls mainly tried to teach their students to be ladies.

Grace played basketball, field hockey, and water polo at Schoonmakers School. Of those school days, Grace recalls, "We had to pass tests to prove we could read, write plain English, and spell. Each summer we had to read twenty books and write reports on them. You were educated and had some background when you were through then, not like today. It didn't give us any inhibitions; it gave us an interest in reading and history."

During her grade school years, Grace received a double promotion. Later however, when it was time to get ready to go to college, she flunked a Latin exam. As a result, Vassar College said she would have to wait a year to enter. Her family also decided Grace was too young to go to Vassar. Grace explains that she didn't like language classes until she learned to read foreign languages and forgot about trying to speak them. Now she can read fluently in the romance languages as well as German and Dutch.

In the fall of 1923, Grace became a boarding student at the Hartridge School in Plainfield, New Jersey. The school was a forty-five-minute train ride from New York City on the Central Railroad of New Jersey.

When Grace attended Hartridge, it was an all-girls school with five resident buildings called the Main House, the Acorn, the Pine Cone, the Mushroom, and the Infirmary. A school catalog from that time assures parents that "all but three bedrooms are corner rooms with cross draughts, and there are only two girls in each room." The school described the climate in Plainfield as exceptionally dry and healthful and their water source as pure.

In addition to an academic curriculum consisting of college

High-button shoes and large hair bows were in style when Grace Murray (third from right), age ten, posed for this photograph with her classmates at the Graham School.

preparatory English, Latin, and one other foreign language such as French, German, or Spanish, a course in history or science was required. Each student also had to participate in singing, calisthenics, gymnastics, aesthetic dancing, and regular exercise.

The school grounds had tennis and basketball courts and a hockey field. In the Recitation Hall, where there were classrooms, there was also a large sports room with bowling alleys and billiard tables. During the winter, the school stage transported students to a skating pond only a few minutes away. Horseback riding lessons were available as well. Each fall there was a tennis tournament. A Field Day of sports and a Riding Exhibition were held in May.

While at Hartridge, Grace was picture editor of a school publication, played hockey and basketball, and was a member of the Glee Club. She also played the part of an Egyptian King in *Miracle Play* and a friar in Shakespeare's *Twelfth Night*.

The 1924 Yearbook from Hartridge placed this quotation next to Grace's graduation picture: "In action faithful and in honor clear."

Miss Emelyn Hartridge, who founded the Hartridge School and taught Latin, was a graduate of Vassar College in Poughkeepsie, New York. She took a personal interest in Grace's talents and encouraged her to continue her education at Vassar. Grace followed this advice and didn't seriously consider any other college. She entered as a freshman in the fall of 1924.

3

The Challenge of Being a College Student

Grace Brewster Murray settled into her seat at the sixty-first con-
vocation of Vassar College. It was Monday, September 22, 1924.
Grace was a newly arrived freshman student, part of the class of
1928. After the undergraduates were in their places, faculty members and the seniors in caps and gowns filed into the chapel in
academic procession.

When everyone was assembled, Dr. Hill of Vassar's Bible
department gave the invocation. Then Dean C. Mildred Thompson
spoke to the students. Her theme, *The Business of Being a Student*,
led her to ask the freshman in the audience, "What does the world
expect of persons between the ages of eighteen and twenty-two?"
Her answer touched on many facets of student life:

> According to the last census there were in this country nearly
> three million young women between the ages of sixteen and
> twenty-four at work to earn their living. In addition to these there
> are millions more who already have taken upon themselves
> family responsibilities. By your very presence here you have
> identified yourselves with the workers and not with the shirkers.
>   We are accustomed to hear that education should be a

preparation for living, but it seems to me that this is only a . . .
partial view . . . . Now you can have more of an experimental
attitude toward living than it may be possible for you to establish
later . . .

Study is not all of college, but . . . it is the most important
business in being a student. You can keep this business as nothing
but a job if you want to; you can work by the time clock and
never do anything more than the least. You may even get an A.B.
degree with this sort of false work; you will cheat yourself most,
but you will cheat others as well.

In contrast to the least student effort, Dean Thompson stated:

You can elevate this business of being a student, if you treat it with
respect and with seriousness and genuine effort, to the dignity of a
profession, and more, if you go at it with joy and with enthusiasm
and give to it the best that is in you, if you let your imagination be
kindled and your spirits moved; then your business of study will
become not merely a profession but it will be to you a great and
lasting adventure . . . . To throw away your opportunities here is an
economic waste. You do not injure yourself alone if you squander
them. If you take advantage of them, you are helping to get your
country ready for whatever future it is to have.

The members of the class of 1928 left the chapel that fall day
each wondering how she would respond to the challenges of the
"business of being a student." But in Grace's mind, there was
determination that she would not waste her life as a student. Her
father and mother had worked hard to offer her this opportunity to
study, and she knew they wanted her to become a self-sufficient
individual. Grace thought that she might become a teacher or an
actuary, a mathematician who analyzes statistics for an insurance
company.

At one time, Grace was approached by one of the professors at
Vassar to help another student who was having difficulty with her
physics course. Under Grace's tutelage, the student went from a *D*

to a passing *C* grade in the subject. What is more important, the experience reinforced Grace's standing among her classmates and professors as a good explainer. She had the qualities of a born teacher.

Grace then tutored groups of students in physics. She was very good at it. For example, if she wanted to teach students about displacement, she didn't just talk about it. She would actually put a fellow student in a partially filled bathtub and mark the rise of the water on the side of the tub! Grace states that she has "always made the connection between the theoretical—the theory itself—and the reality. That's the way you explain things."

When Grace attended Vassar, students could audit as many courses as they wanted in addition to the ones for which they were formally registered. During her four years at Vassar, Grace audited all of the beginning courses in each of the sciences, including botany, physiology, and geology. In the same manner, she also took

Grace Murray as a student at Vassar College in 1928.

courses in business and economics. She was hungry to learn as much as she could.

Grace says there were no engineering courses for women then, so she registered to take mathematics and physics. She took a course in electricity that included optics and built a spectroscope. A course in electronics covered ions, electrons, and ionizing radiation.

Besides her academic work, Grace was involved in a number of other activities at Vassar. She played basketball and took part in other sports. She also talked the school administrators into donating the necessary paint and organized a group of students to paint the inside of the old physics laboratory that was in need of improvement.

For two years, Grace and her sister were at Vassar together. During that time Grace got her involved in making costumes for a Spanish play, among other activities.

Vassar had built-in good times, such as Founder's Day in the

Main building at Vassar College, Poughkeepsie, New York.

spring. Each Founder's Day had a theme, and usually a picnic was held on the campus. President Henry MacCracken and the students traditionally sang "Camptown Races" together. There was an afternoon baseball game and a faculty-student play in the evening. The whole event was great fun.

On some Saturday afternoons, tea dances were held to which the students at Vassar invited fellows. The young women wore fancy gowns and white gloves. The young men came in evening dress, or if they were from West Point, they wore their handsome uniforms. The Vassar students tried to dance with each other's dates, to make them feel welcome and popular. The dances were from 4:00 P.M. to midnight because the student building where they were held had been donated by a man who didn't think it was proper to dance on Sundays.

Grace Hopper has always loved adventure. She recalls that when she was eighteen, a barnstorming biplane made of "wood,

Photograph of Grace Brewster Murray as it appeared in the Vassar Yearbook in 1928.

linen, and wire" landed in a field near Vassar. "It had one engine and an open cockpit so you got the full benefit of the wind," said Grace. "I squandered all my money—it cost $10—and went up in the plane."

Grace Murray graduated from Vassar College in 1928 with a Bachelor of Arts degree in mathematics and physics. During her senior year at Vassar, she was elected to Phi Beta Kappa, the oldest honor society in the United States. Grace also won a Vassar College Fellowship, a scholarship that allowed her to go on with her education. Without it, her sister Mary says, Grace may not have continued in school for fear of putting too much of a financial burden on her parents, who had Mary's and Roger's schooling to consider as well.

Grace attended Yale University, where her roommate gave her a Boston Terrier, a pet she kept for ten years. In 1930, Grace received a Master of Arts degree in mathematics. At Yale, she was invited to join Sigma Xi, an honor society that recognizes scientists for their outstanding research achievements.

4

Marriage and a Teaching Career

In 1930, Grace Murray married Vincent Foster Hopper. She had met him in Wolfeboro the summer before he entered Princeton University. Vincent was the son of Mrs. Abram Whitaker Hopper and the late Rev. Dr. Hopper, who had been the rector of Trinity Reformed Church at West New York, New Jersey.

The wedding took place on the evening of June 15, 1930, at West End Collegiate Church. The ceremony was performed by the Rev. Dr. Henry Evertson Cobb, assisted by the Rev. Dr. John Y. Broek, of Plainfield, New Jersey. Grace's parents had been married by Dr. Cobb in the same church in 1903.

Mary Murray, who had graduated from Vassar College with a major in economics the weekend before the wedding, was her sister's maid of honor. Her brother, then a student at Yale University, was best man. After the wedding, guests attended a reception and dinner held at the Savoy Plaza.

Vincent Foster Hopper had graduated from Princeton University in 1927 with highest honors, having been elected to Phi Beta Kappa in his junior year. He received his Master of Arts degree from Princeton in 1928. At the time of his marriage to Grace, he was an instructor in English at New York University's School of Commerce. Later, he studied for a doctoral degree in Comparative Literature at Columbia University, which he attained in 1938.

Within a week after the wedding, the couple set sail for Europe together with Grace's family. They landed at Cherbourg, France, and from there embarked on a motor trip through Europe. The whole family also went to Wales, Scotland, and England before coming back to the United States in September. Grace particularly recalls visiting Stonehenge for the first time. It is her favorite monument in the world. When Grace and Vincent returned, they made their home in New York City.

The newlyweds were married during an era known as the Great Depression. General economic activity was very slow, many people were out of work, and jobs were hard to find, even for well-educated people. When Vassar offered Grace a position teaching mathematics at $800 a year, she jumped at the chance.

As a new faculty member, Grace started out teaching algebra, trigonometry, and calculus. Later she developed theory of probability, statistics, and analysis courses. Grace Murray Hopper was a faculty member in the Mathematics Department of her alma mater from 1931 until 1943, during which time she rose from instructor to associate professor.

In 1934 Grace Hopper received a Ph.D. from Yale and was awarded two Sterling scholarships. As part of the work for her advanced degree, she had completed a dissertation entitled "The Irreducibility of Algebraic Equations."

In the 1930s a doctorate in mathematics was a rare accomplishment for anyone. In the three years following Grace's graduation, Yale awarded only seven Ph.D.s in mathematics. During the time Grace was working on her doctorate, there were less than ten doctoral students in mathematics at Yale and four of them were women. For a woman to achieve one of these degrees, therefore, was truly remarkable. Even today, not many women receive a doctorate in this field.

Winifred Asprey is a member of the class of 1938 at Vassar College and a former student of Grace Hopper's. She took all of Dr. Hopper's classes and describes her as a serious and outstanding teacher. Although Grace Hopper knew all of her students well, she and Winifred Asprey became particularly close friends. Later, Winifred became chairman of the Mathematics Department at Vassar College. In 1954 and 1955, when Vassar installed a computer center, Winifred Asprey consulted with Grace Hopper about the project.

This photograph taken in the mid-1930s shows a youthful and attractive Dr. Hopper.

Another student from Grace Hopper's Vassar teaching days is Professor Anne O'Neill. She took several courses with Dr. Hopper, including geometry, calculus, and mechanical drawing. To this day, Anne O'Neill thinks of Dr. Hopper as a very vibrant teacher and says that Grace Hopper certainly influenced her to go on to get a Ph.D. in mathematics. Dr. O'Neill is now a Professor Emeritus at Wheaton College in Norton, Massachusetts.

In 1939 Grace and Vincent Hopper built a traditional two-story home in Poughkeepsie. To accommodate visits by Grace's father, who had difficulty climbing stairs, the house was designed with a bedroom and bath on the first floor. Another bath and more bedrooms were located on the second floor.

In addition to the living quarters, there was a garage for a Model A Ford roadster. Grace dubbed the Model A "Dr. Johnson" after Dr. Samuel Johnson of literary fame. She chose this name because in her youth she had used a quotation from Dr. Johnson regularly. At Lake Wentworth, whenever Grace jumped into the water from the dock for a swim, she quoted Dr. Johnson: "I despise immersion." She explained, "That car never got washed."

Vincent continued to teach at New York University where he specialized in Renaissance literature. Each weekend he made the two-hour commute by train back and forth between Poughkeepsie and New York City.

Grace was awarded a Vassar faculty fellowship and chose to study at the Courant Institute of New York University from 1941 to 1942. In 1943 she also taught for a short time at Barnard College.

5

Grace Joins the WAVES

The United States was catapulted into World War II when the Japanese attacked Pearl Harbor, a United States naval base in Hawaii, on December 7, 1941. The losses of military personnel, aircraft, and ships were catastrophic, and the surprise attack galvanized the American people into action. Grace Hopper recalls that she was sitting at her desk in her home in Poughkeepsie correcting school papers when the philharmonic concert on the radio was interrupted by the announcement that Pearl Harbor had been bombed.

On December 8, one day before Grace Murray Hopper's thirty-fifth birthday, President Franklin D. Roosevelt arose at dawn to complete drafting his speech to the United States Congress asking for a declaration of war against Japan. His famous war message began, "Yesterday, December 7, 1941—a date which will live in infamy—the United States of America was suddenly and deliberately attacked by naval and air forces of the Empire of Japan."

The United States had tried to stay out of the war for as long as possible. But as President Roosevelt expressed in his address, "The facts of yesterday speak for themselves. The people of the United

States have already formed their opinions and well understand the implications to the very life and safety of our nation."

He went on to say, "With confidence in our armed forces—with the unbounding determination of our people—we will gain the inevitable triumph—so help us God."

Ending his speech, the President stated, "I ask that the Congress declare that since the unprovoked and dastardly attack by Japan on Sunday, December 7th, a state of war has existed between the United States and the Japanese Empire."

Germany, under the rule of Adolf Hitler, had been pursuing world conquest in Europe. As had been expected for a long time, on December 11, 1941, Germany and its ally Italy declared war against the United States. Never in the history of the world had there been a greater threat to freedom, civilization, and our nation.

President Roosevelt requested the Congress to recognize also a state of war between the United States and Germany and the United States and Italy on December 11, 1941.

World War II was a difficult time filled with intense patriotism for all Americans. Both Grace's husband and her brother joined the United States Army Air Forces as volunteers under the draft. Grace's father served on the Selective Service Board, her mother on the Ration Board, and her sister worked in a big General Electric plant making proximity fuses. (A proximity fuse is a device that sets off a bomb as it nears its target.) As Grace put it, "Everyone joined something."

When people say to Grace Hopper that women have never been recognized in this country, she replies, "What about Rosie the Riveter?" Rosie represented over three million American women homemakers who went to work in the defense factories of the United States during World War II. It was these women, often working long hours in dangerous, dirty jobs, who built the ships, the aircraft, the tanks, and the guns to help their country win World War II.

Women riveting a bomber fuselage in a defense plant during World War II.
Rosie-the-Riveter came to represent all of these women whose efforts helped win
the war.

Rationing became another part of the war effort. There were shortages of sugar, flour, butter, meat, and gasoline. The railroads were so busy moving military equipment that they couldn't always carry these commodities to where they were needed. Coupons were issued by the government that allotted individuals and families only so much of items in short supply.

During the war, when you walked around in a big city like New York, "There was a certain age group that just wasn't there," said Grace Hopper.

Deeply affected by the war, Grace took it as a personal challenge; a job that had to be tackled. Another event in Grace's life was also influencing her. In the early 1940s, Grace and Vincent Hopper separated. They had had no children. Later, in 1945, they divorced.

Grace wanted to join the United States Navy. However, she was considered overage for enlistment and, as a mathematics professor, worked at an occupation that had been classified by United States government officials as crucial. Mathematicians could best serve the war effort as civilians, they felt.

Only two ways were available for Grace Hopper to join the Navy. She either had to resign her teaching position and remain out of work for six months or she could try to get special permission. She managed to get permission—and a leave of absence from her faculty position at Vassar by threatening to quit.

But then came another hurdle. The Navy regulations stated that she was supposed to weigh at least 121 pounds for her height of five feet six inches. Grace weighed only 105 pounds. Again she was able to get a waiver.

Grace Murray Hopper was sworn into the United States Naval Reserve in December of 1943.

When asked why she joined the Naval Reserve, Grace exclaimed, "There was a war on! It was not unusual for a woman at that time to join the Navy; there were 30,000 to 40,000 women there at the time." She further explained, "It was the only thing to do."

Grace's family had always served their country—from the American Revolution on. One of her ancestors was a Minute Man. Her great-grandfather on her mother's side, Alexander Wilson Russell, had been a rear admiral in the Navy. She recalls meeting him: "I was about three years old when I first met him. Although long retired, he was tall and straight, carried a black cane with a silver top on it, and had white muttonchop whiskers, which I had never seen before. He was a very impressive gentleman!"

During World War I, women performed yeoman duties such as clerical and secretarial tasks for the United States Navy to relieve enlisted men for active duty, but they were barred from joining the regular Navy. It was not until World War II that Congress established the Women's Reserve of the United States Naval Reserve. Mildred H. McAfee, an educator, served as the first director of the WAVES (Women Accepted for Volunteer Emergency Service). By August 1945, as World War II neared an end, the peak strength of the WAVES was attained with 86,000 women in service.

After enlistment, Grace underwent training at the United States Naval Reserve Midshipman's School for Women in Northampton, Massachusetts. For Grace, this was a make-or-break time. If she did not graduate from Midshipman's School, she would be out of the Navy.

In addition, when Grace Hopper arrived at Midshipman's School, she found that she was in the same class as the students she had been teaching at Vassar. Compared to Grace, the others in her battalion were "youngsters." There was no doubt that she faced heavy pressure.

The day at Midshipman's School started at the crack of dawn. Grace's battalion was housed in the old Northampton Hotel and hence was known as the hotel battalion. Another battalion lived on the campus of Smith College. In Grace's battalion, four women slept in a room. Each person had to keep her possessions in a suitcase under her bunk.

Grace remembers that the sheets on the bunks had to be absolutely tight. At first, they were tested by throwing a nickel on the bunk. If the coin bounced, the sheets were judged tight enough. Later, the sheets were tested with a quarter. Another tough job for Grace and the other enlisted women was keeping their shoes shined, no matter what the weather.

After an early breakfast, the battalion marched to the campus. There they were given courses in Navy orientation. Grace says these included, "What is the Navy?, What's it like?, naval history, naval customs and usages—in short everything about the Navy. The students also had courses in the recognition of ships and aircraft. Outlines of ships and aircraft were flashed on a screen, and the students had to identify them. Grace kept mixing up the carriers and the submarines. "You'd be surprised how, held down on the horizon, a submarine on the surface can look very much like a carrier," explains Grace.

The battalion underwent drill on campus and marched in all kinds of formations. In the afternoon, the students had physical education. All in all, it was a long day, and then there were assignments to read at night.

While Grace was at Midshipman's School, D-Day, one of the most extraordinary and daring military operations in history, took place in Europe. On June 6, 1944, the Allied Forces invaded the continent of Europe along the beaches of Normandy, France. Grace remembers that everyone at Midshipman's School went to a special service at the chapel. To this day, Grace Hopper says she wears her uniform every year on June 6 and on December 7.

After she completed her training, Grace graduated first in her class from Midshipman's School. She was commissioned a lieutenant (junior grade) on June 27, 1944. Grace says that when she was commissioned, she took a sheath of flowers to her great-grandfather Alexander Wilson Russell's grave and told him it was "all right for females to be Navy officers."

The Navy immediately assigned Grace to work at the Bureau of Ordnance Computation Project at Harvard University. The assignment would change the course of her career.

6

Enter Howard Aiken and the Mark I

During the seven-year period from 1937 to 1944, events at Harvard University had led to the creation of a new kind of calculating machine that would capture Grace Hopper's imagination and make challenging use of her training in mathematics and physics.

The idea to build the Mark I computer might not have been explored at the time, but Howard Aiken had come to Harvard University to earn his Ph.D., and the research he was doing for his doctorate involved a massive amount of time-consuming calculations. He began looking for a way to do the long and tedious calculations by machine. In doing so, Aiken was following in the footsteps of an Englishman, Charles Babbage.

Charles Babbage lived from 1791 to 1871. Babbage is known today as the father of the computer because, in his lifetime, he designed and tried to build machines that would do complex calculations.

Babbage's ideas forecast those used in today's computers. His "analytical engine," as he called one of his machines, had two separate parts. The first was called the "store," and it held the numbers that were to be used in the calculation. Babbage called the

Portrait of Charles Babbage taken in 1860.

second part of the engine the "mill," and it performed the calculations.

The steps or order of the operations for a calculation on Babbage's analytical engine were controlled by the use of punched cards. The idea to use punched cards was borrowed from Jacquard looms, which were in use in Europe at that time. These looms controlled the patterns woven into cloth with cards that had holes punched in them. By varying the pattern of the holes punched in the cards controlling a Jacquard loom, different patterns could be woven into the cloth a loom produced.

Unfortunately, Charles Babbage lived before the proper machine tools, materials, and electrical circuits were available to successfully build and operate his engine. As he stated in his *Life of a Philosopher*, published in 1864, "If, unwarned by my example, any man shall . . . succeed in really constructing an engine . . . of mathematical analysis upon different principles or by simpler mechanical means, I have no fear of leaving my reputation in his charge, for he alone will be fully able to appreciate the nature of my efforts and the value of their results."

Babbage's work was noticed and appreciated by Ada Byron Lovelace, the daughter of England's famous poet Lord Byron. Ada Lovelace was a mathematical genius who recognized and understood the importance of Babbage's work. She wrote detailed descriptions of his plans for an analytical engine and how it would operate.

Ada Lovelace also noted that certain operations were often repeated in doing complex calculations and devised a method to automatically repeat those steps on the analytical engine when needed in a calculation. Thus Ada Lovelace is thought of today as the first computer programmer. The Pentagon has named a universal standard computer language Ada, in honor of Ada Lovelace.

In 1937, Howard Aiken wrote a memo entitled "Proposed Automatic Calculating Machine." The paper described the calculating machine that Aiken wanted to build. It was the first large-scale digital computer. Two Harvard professors, Dr. Harlow Shapley and Professor T. H. Brown, read the paper and advised Aiken to talk with the president of International Business Machines, Thomas Watson, Sr. A meeting between Aiken and Watson resulted in a signed contract in 1939.

IBM and the Harvard Research Facility would cooperate to construct the Automatic Sequence Controlled Calculator (ASCC), also known as the Mark I computer. The computer would be the joint product of Aiken's ideas—what he wanted the machine to be able to do—and the technology available at IBM at that time. The Mark I computer was built at the IBM laboratories in Endicott, New York, under the direction of Clair D. Lake and two associates there, Frank D. Hamilton and Benjamin M. Durfee. Patent number 2,616,626 for the design of the machine names Aiken, Lake, Hamilton, and Durfee as co-inventors.

The Mark I was tested successfully on its first problem in January 1943. Complete testing was finished in the IBM Laboratory in Endicott. In December 1943, the computer was demonstrated there to Dr. James Bryant Conant, president of Harvard, and to other university faculty.

The Mark I was then disassembled and moved to a specially constructed room in the Cruft Laboratory at Harvard. There it was reassembled and given final tests. IBM's president, Thomas Watson, Sr., gave the Mark I to Harvard University as a gift from IBM at the official dedication of the computer on August 7, 1944. The computer was the fulfillment of Charles Babbage's dream, over one hundred years after his death.

The Mark I was eight feet high, eight feet deep, and had a rotary shaft running its fifty-one foot length. The shaft was driven by a four-horsepower motor located between two panels that extended at right angles from the back of the computer. The five-ton Mark I had about 800,000 parts and over 500 miles of wire.

The glass-encased computer was electromechanical, not electronic. That is, it was run by electricity, but contained a mountain of large, bulky mechanical switches or relays that opened and closed during its operation. The relays did the same job inside the computer that vacuum tubes, transistors, or microchips would do in later years in more modern computers.

When the Mark I was performing a calculation, the opening and closing of the relays made a clacking noise that sounded like a roomful of people knitting.

The computer's 3,300 relays could handle numbers up to twenty-three digits in length, plus an algebraic sign for positive or

The Mark I computer at the Cruft Laboratory, Harvard University.

negative numbers. The Mark I had sixty registers, or sets of switches that were individually set by hand for the input of constants (numbers that do not change value during a mathematical calculation). There were seventy-two storage registers for the addition of numbers and a central multiplication and division unit. The Mark I also could compute mathematical functions such as logarithms and sines.

The Mark I used continuous punched IBM card stock for input and IBM electric typewriters for output of printed information.

The automatic sequence of steps in a calculation on the Mark I was controlled by instructions encoded as punched holes on a paper tape. Each line on the tape had space for twenty-four (three groups of eight) punched holes. Each line represented a single command to the computer.

The Mark I could perform three additions every second. It was heralded as a modern mechanical miracle. Calculations that would have taken six months to do by hand now were being done in one day.

The Mark I was flexible and useful enough to stay in service until 1959. It was well suited to the computation of tables. When it was retired, the Mark I was dismantled. Parts of the computer can be seen at Harvard University in Cambridge, Massachusetts, IBM headquarters in New York, and at the Smithsonian Institution in Washington, D.C.

As Grace Hopper has said, "It [the Mark I] was man's first attempt to build a machine that would assist the power of his brain rather than the strength of his arm."

7

Grace Hopper Meets the Mark I

By the time the finishing touches were being applied to the Mark I, Lieutenant Grace Murray Hopper was ready for work at the Bureau of Ordnance Computation Project. "I'd never thought of going into computer work because there weren't any computers to go into—except for the Mark I, which I didn't know anything about," says Grace. "In the 1940s, you know, you could have put all the computer people in the country into one small room."

After a weekend with her family, Grace Hopper went to Boston to report for work on Monday, July 2, 1944. She has described that day many times.

First Grace went to headquarters, where she was told to go out to Harvard. Several hours later, about two o'clock in the afternoon, Grace found where she was supposed to be. The Bureau of Ordnance Computation Project was in the basement of Cruft Laboratory.

When Grace walked in the door, Commander Aiken looked up and said, "Where the hell have you been?"

Grace thought Commander Aiken was referring to her two days

off and the fact that she had spent much of the day trying to find the place. So she tried to explain all that.

Then Howard Aiken said, "I mean for the last two months!"

Grace replied that she had been at Midshipman's school.

Aiken said, "I told them you didn't need that; we've got to get to work." He then waved his hand at the Mark I and said, "That's a computing engine."

For the first time, Grace Hopper saw the Mark I computer, all fifty-one feet of it.

Grace received her first assignment right away. Commander Aiken informed her that he "would be delighted to have the coefficients for the interpolation of the arc tangent by next Thursday."

Two young ensigns, Robert V. D. Campbell and Richard M. Bloch, rescued Grace.

Commander Howard Aiken (center front row) with Navy crew members at the Harvard Computation Laboratory about 1944. Lieutenant Grace M. Hopper is next to him. Robert V.D. Campbell is next to Grace, and Richard M. Bloch is on the other end of the front row.

Grace learned that the two ensigns had heard a white-haired old schoolteacher was coming and that they had bribed each other as to who would sit next to her. But as Grace says, "They were most kind to me, and they did help me get my first program onto the computer, which computed the coefficients of the arc tangent interpolation function."

Years later, when Grace Hopper again met Bob Campbell and Dick Bloch, they talked about how they used to troubleshoot the Mark I. When they suspected a relay had failed, they would turn out the lights and go behind the front panel of the computer. Grace would use a purse-sized mirror to locate telltale sparks from the relay that had faltered.

Grace fell in love with the Mark I on sight. She didn't say so to Howard Aiken that very first day at Harvard, but all she could think was, "Gee, that's the prettiest gadget I ever saw." She still thinks of the huge old Mark I as her favorite computer and sometimes visits the Mark I at the Smithsonian.

8

Grace's Early Days as a Programmer

Grace Hopper was only the third person to program the Mark I, the world's first large-scale automatically sequenced digital computer. Programming was called coding then. The word *programming* was used by the British, who were busy building their own computers, and it was not until several years later that the term came into common use in the United States. Grace Hopper says, "American computer people finally adopted the term because, I think, it sounded elegant and they thought that 'programmers' would make more money than 'coders.'"

An associate professor of mathematics in the Graduate School of Engineering at Harvard University, Howard Aiken also was a commander in the United States Naval Reserve. He ran the bureau's operations like a Navy ship. Aiken used nautical terms and kept a logbook. He was a very important person in Grace Hopper's professional life and an outstanding model for her.

Grace Hopper says Howard Aiken was "just terrific. He was a real leader and he got the best out of everybody. We all worshiped him. The only real predecessor of Aiken's concept [for the computer] was Babbage." Grace Hopper says Aiken was "The real pioneer . . . . I don't think Aiken's ever been given the credit for the first large-scale digital computer, even if it was built out of step counters and relays." He wrote some of the earliest codes to program the Mark I.

By the time the Mark I was dedicated at Harvard University, World War II had made vital finding a way to quickly compute the complex calculations necessary to accurately aim new Navy guns. The United States Navy Bureau of Ships leased the Mark I for the remainder of the war to do the job.

The computer was operated around the clock to provide the calculations that Navy gunners needed during wartime. Aiming one of the new Navy guns required knowing the angle necessary to elevate the gun from the horizon of the earth in order to hit a target at a known distance from the gunner. A gunner also had to consider crosswinds, air density and temperature, and the weight of the shell.

"There was a rush on everything, and we didn't realize what was really happening," recalls Grace Hopper. "All of a sudden we had self-propelled rockets, and we had to compute where they were going and what they were going to do. The development of the atomic bomb also required a tremendous amount of computation, as did acoustic and magnetic mines."

The crew running the Mark I computer consisted of Grace Hopper, three other officers, and four enlisted men. They had the responsibility to keep the computer running twenty-four hours a day. Grace remembers that she and other crew members often would sleep on their desks to be on the spot should the computer run into difficulties. If they went home to sleep, they might be routed out of bed at any hour to fix the computer and complete much-needed calculations.

An example of the kind of problem that she was asked to solve using the Mark I computer was to calculate the area covered by a mine-sweeping detector towed behind a ship. The Mark I was used to calculate not only logistics and firing tables for guns but also a top secret mathematical simulation of the shock waves that would result when the first atomic bomb was exploded.

Grace Hopper recounts what it was like to work for Howard Aiken, "It was a challenge. You could make any mistake in the world once, but not twice." She also describes Howard Aiken as a good teacher who led her and others to go on in the field of computing.

She adds," He [Aiken] was a tough taskmaster. I was sitting at my desk one day, and he came up behind me, and I got to my feet real fast, and he said, 'You're going to write a book.' I said, 'I can't write a book!' He said, 'You're in the Navy now.' So I wrote a book."

The book was "A Manual of Operation for the Automatic Sequence Controlled Calculator," published in the *Annals of the Harvard Computation Laboratory*, Volume I, Harvard University Press, 1946. The foreword of the book was written by James Bryant Conant, who was president of Harvard University from 1933 to 1953. During World War II, Dr. Conant also worked as a science adviser for the United States government's Office of Scientific Research.

In the foreword, Dr. Conant said, "No combination of printed words can ever do justice to the real story of an undertaking in which cooperation between men of capacity and genius is of the essence. The development of the IBM Automatic Sequence Controlled Calculator is such a story, with many fascinating chapters."

In addition, President Conant stated, "On August 7, 1944, Mr. Thomas J. Watson, on behalf of the International Business Machines Corporation, presented Harvard University with the IBM Automatic Sequence Controlled Calculator. Since that date the machine has been in constant use by the Navy Department on confidential work. Therefore, Mr. Watson's gift came at a time when the new instrument his company had created was able to serve the country in time of war . . . ."

Thomas J. Watson, Sr., president of IBM Corporation.

9

The Harvard Computers

Like any computer, the Mark I was essentially a huge number of switches. To program it, instructions had to be written in a machine code that told the computer exactly what operations it must perform and in what sequence or order to do them for a calculation. The instructions detailed which switches in the computer were to be set at either an ON or an OFF position.

The Mark I computer understood only one language—a machine language that consisted of code numbers. The code numbers told the computer how to perform a particular calculation. The Mark I was a one-of-a-kind machine, and a new program representing a different pattern of codes had to be written for each task or problem to be solved.

To program the Mark I Grace Hopper says, "The coding sheets we used had three columns on the left [for code numbers] and we wrote comments on the right which didn't go into the computer." Holes were punched into paper tape that stood for the code numbers on the coding sheets. Each horizontal line of holes on the paper tape represented a single command. In general each command stated,

"Take the number out of unit A; deliver it to unit B; start operation C."

An example of a single command is seen on the seventh line of the control tape shown in the photograph. The code number in the first column tells the computer to take the quantity out of register 321, in the second column 761 means deliver the quantity from register 321 into the multiplier, and 732 in the third column means take a negative or multiply by minus the contents of register 321.

When programming an early computer, it was quite easy to make errors. The machine language of code numbers readily could be misread or copied incorrectly. As Grace described it: "You write 'B' and someone reads it as '13.'" Or "You write a Delta [a mathematical symbol shaped like a triangle] and someone reads it as a 'four.' And sometimes you just make a mistake and write the wrong thing to begin with."

As time passed, Howard Aiken developed a habit of coming into the laboratory where Grace and others were working and asking, "Are you making any numbers?" The programmers were always searching for some reason to give if they were not "making any numbers" at that moment.

One warm day in 1945 the programmers were provided with an answer they would use again and again. By this time, the Mark II, the successor to the Mark I, was under construction in the laboratory.

Grace Hopper recounts, "In the summer of 1945 we were building the Mark II; we had to build it in an awful rush—it was wartime—out of components we could get our hands on." Grace and the rest of the crew were working in a temporary building constructed during World War I. All the windows were open because it was a hot summer and there was no air-conditioning to relieve the oppressive heat.

Suddenly, the Mark II stopped. After a while, the crew found

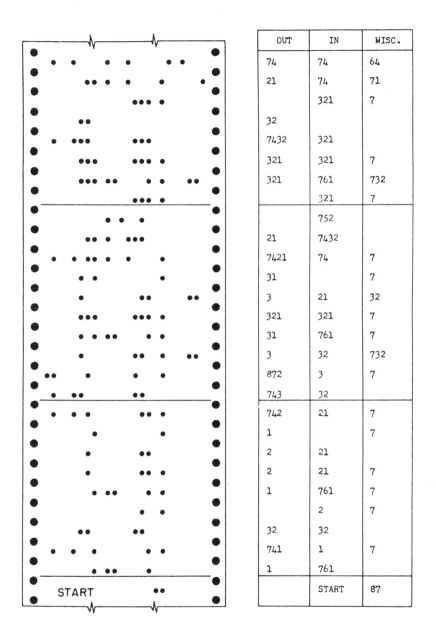

OUT	IN	MISC.
74	74	64
21	74	71
	321	7
32		
7432	321	
321	321	7
321	761	732
	321	7
	752	
21	7432	
7421	74	7
31		7
3	21	32
321	321	7
31	761	7
3	32	732
872	3	7
743	32	
742	21	7
1		7
2	21	
2	21	7
1	761	7
	2	7
32	32	
741	1	7
1	761	
	START	87

An example of the coding sheet for the Mark I.

57

the relay that had failed. Inside the relay was a moth that had been beaten to death by the relay.

Grace says, "We got a pair of tweezers. Very carefully we took the moth out of the relay, put it in the logbook, and put scotch tape over it . . . . From then on if we weren't making any numbers, we told him [Aiken] that we were debugging the computer." As far as Grace knows, that's where the term *debugging* started. The first bug still exists in the logbook kept at the Naval Museum at the Naval Surface Weapons Center in Dahlgren, Virginia.

The Mark II computer was designed, built, and tested for the Navy Bureau of Ordnance within three years and was five times faster than the Mark I. It was installed at the Naval Proving Ground in Dahlgren.

Grace Hopper tells us that the Mark II was the first multiprocessor. Under program control "you could split it into two computers, side by side. It worked in parallel and exchanged data through the transfer registers. And then under program control you could throw it back into being one computer again. So it was the beginning of multiprocessors," says Grace. "Aiken's never been given credit for Mark II, which was a parallel processor."

Grace and her fellow workers at Harvard began to collect pieces of code that they knew were correct and that worked. "When we got a correct subroutine, a piece of a program that had been checked out and debugged—one that we knew worked—we put it in a notebook," says Grace.

This method eventually led Grace and the others on the crew to borrow pieces of code from each other for programs they knew worked. For example, there was a debugged piece of code or subroutine for finding the sine, one for finding the cosine, one for finding the arc tangent, and one for integrating something. All of these subroutines used numbers and mathematical symbols only. They were very helpful for scientific or mathematical problems, but were not something a person unfamiliar with mathematics could use.

Grace wanted to stay in the Navy, which now allowed women in the WAVES to transfer to the regular Navy. However, she had turned forty and the maximum allowable age was thirty-eight. As Grace has said, "That was the first time I was told I was too old. . . I always explain to everybody it's better to be told you're too old when you're forty because then you go through the experience and it doesn't bother you again."

Though Grace had an offer to return to Vassar to teach mathematics as a full professor, she instead decided to stay at the Harvard

Page from logbook showing "First actual case of bug being found."

Computation Laboratory as a Research Fellow in Engineering Sciences and Applied Physics. The Mark III was being developed, and Grace "decided that computers were more fun."

Grace also decided to stay in the Naval Reserve, where she took ordnance courses and War College courses. The War College courses included solving problems such as fueling a task force at sea in minimum time when given the rates that different ships could pump oil and receive oil. Other problems involved scouting the Caribbean with a squadron of submarines in minimum time or making a plan to take an island.

The building of the Mark III computer was started in 1948, again for the United States Navy. This computer used vacuum tubes and magnetic tapes for higher speed input and output. The Mark III was fifty times faster than the Mark I. It also was sent to the Naval Proving Ground in Dahlgren to join the Mark II in doing ballistic calculations. Both computers were in operation until 1955.

The Air Force backed the construction of the Mark IV and placed it in service in 1952 at Harvard University. The Mark IV was three times faster than the Mark III and one hundred and fifty times faster than the original computer of the series, the Mark I. The Mark IV was the last in the Harvard series of Automatic Sequence Controlled Calculators and was in service until 1962.

10

Taking Risks at the Forefront of a New Industry

In 1949, Grace Hopper left Harvard University and joined the Eckert-Mauchly Computer Corporation in Philadelphia as senior mathematician. This move was not without risk.

Most people involved with the design and building of electronic computers in the late 1940s thought that there would be no need for computers in large numbers. They believed that the computers currently under construction in England and in America would be all that were needed worldwide for at least the next ten years.

Even IBM agreed with this shortsighted view. Nonscientific and business applications of the power of computers were not considered as necessities. Grace Hopper has said, "Back in those days, everybody was using punched cards, and they thought they'd use punched cards forever." To believe otherwise went against the established thinking of the time. However, Grace Hopper had dared to take risks since childhood, and she saw a business future for computers.

Howard Aiken, John Mauchly, and J. Presper Eckert also envisioned greater future business applications for computers. After World War II, Aiken tried to get the Prudential Life Insurance

61

Company to use the Mark I to produce premium notices. Grace Hopper recalls that Aiken believed a computer would one day fit into a shoebox (thus making it more accessible for business use). Not many people agreed with him at the time.

During World War II, J. Presper Eckert and John Mauchly built the world's first general-purpose electronic computer at the University of Pennsylvania's Moore School of Electrical Engineering. It was known as ENIAC, shorthand for Electronic Numerical Integrator and Calculator. ENIAC was over one hundred feet long and ten feet high, weighed over thirty tons, and housed over 18,000 glass electronic vacuum tubes. It took over two and a half years to

A partial view of ENIAC with J. Presper Eckert at the controls.

assemble. ENIAC used so much power, approximately 200 kilowatts, that it was rumored every time the computer was turned on, the lights in Philadelphia dimmed.

About two years before ENIAC was unveiled to the public, Eckert, Mauchly, and their staff already were thinking about ENIAC's successor, EDVAC, or Electronic Discrete Variable Automatic Computer. EDVAC was not completed until 1952, but the concepts used to build it became the foundation of most of the major first-generation computers from which the computers of today arose.

The EDVAC was very different from ENIAC. EDVAC had a much larger memory and was built as a binary machine. ENIAC was a decimal machine, using the familiar decimal number system we use every day. Each decimal digit was represented by a ring of ten flip-flop switches inside the computer. EDVAC, on the other hand, as a binary machine, used a number system based on two digits, 0 and 1. For these reasons, EDVAC could be constructed using only a fraction of the number of electronic vacuum tubes in ENIAC.

The larger memory of EDVAC also made possible internal control of the sequence of steps in the operation of the computer. Instructions to do a calculation were held in the computer's memory along with the numbers needed for the computation.

Internal control was a major improvement over the use of external control. ENIAC required the handsetting of hundreds of switches and plugs and sockets before it could perform a calculation. Other computers used punched paper tape or cards to instruct the computer about the sequence of steps in a calculation. A program of instructions stored inside the computer would greatly reduce the setup time needed before performing lengthy calculations.

The plans for the design of EDVAC were published widely and

THE DECIMAL, BINARY, AND OCTAL NUMBER SYSTEMS

A feature of each number system is its *base*. The base is the number of digits that are used to stand for quantities in a number system. For example, in the decimal number system the base is ten because the ten digits 0 through 9 are used to represent all numbers in the system.

The binary number system has a base of two because it uses only two digits, 0 and 1, to represent all numbers in the system. The octal number system has a base of eight because it uses eight digits, 0 through 7, to represent all numbers in the system.

Some Decimal Numbers Compared to Numbers Written in Binary or Octal:

Decimal Number	Binary Number	Octal Number
0	0	0
1	1	1
2	10	2
3	11	3
4	100	4
5	101	5
6	110	6
7	111	7
8	1000	10
9	1001	11
10	1010	12
11	1011	13
12	1100	14
13	1101	15
14	1110	16
15	1111	17
16	10000	20
17	10001	21
18	10010	22
19	10011	23
20	10100	24

affected the thinking of many people who were involved in projects to build computers in the late 1940s.

Eckert and Mauchly left the Moore School in 1946 and founded their own computer company. Their first job was to build a computer for Northrop Aircraft Corporation. It was to be used for a secret project known as the Snark Missile project. The computer that the company built was called BINAC, or Binary Automatic Computer. Just as it was being completed, Grace Murray Hopper joined the company.

BINAC was sent to Northrop in the middle of 1949. Grace Hopper was one of a small team who traveled to Hawthorne, California, to teach Northrop employees how to use the computer.

The experience gained in building BINAC was used by Eckert and Mauchly to design and build the first mass-produced commercial computer in 1951. UNIVAC I, or Universal Automatic Computer, had many memory devices, including storage tubes and magnetic cores. It also used high-speed magnetic tape instead of punched cards to record data.

John Mauchly wrote the C-10 code for the UNIVAC I. According to Grace Hopper, the C-10 code "has been the basis of most codes since. A was add, M was multiply, B was bring, C was clear; it was a beautiful code. That instruction has been the foundation of every instruction code since. The logic of UNIVAC I was Mauchly's." Grace adds, "The logic, the design, how the data flowed, how the instructions operated, and everything else was Mauchly's."

"Those were precarious days," Grace Hopper remembers. "We used to say that if UNIVAC I didn't work, we were going to throw it out one side of the factory, which was a junkyard, and we were going to jump out the other side, which was a cemetery!"

As things turned out, the UNIVAC computer was a great success. It was much smaller than its predecessors—only fourteen and one-half feet long, nine feet wide, and seven and one-half feet high.

Its memory could hold 1,000 machine language "words." It processed 3,000 additions or subtractions each second, a full one thousand times faster than the Mark I. It used magnetic tape for storing, processing, and receiving information.

UNIVAC became so well known that its name practically had the same meaning to people as the generic word *computer*.

11

Early Steps in Developing Programming Languages

When Grace Hopper programmed the BINAC, she used a short code that John Mauchly had developed to serve as an interpreter for that computer. The BINAC was programmed in octal, a mathematical system based on the numbers 0 through 7, a total of eight digits.

Grace recalls that she taught herself to add, subtract, multiply, and divide in octal. She says, "I was really good." There was only one problem. Grace's checkbook was out of balance at the end of the month. It remained out of balance for three months until her brother, who is a banker, checked her account and informed her that every once in a while she had subtracted in octal.

Mauchly's short code was an attempt to create instructions that would allow the computer to accept mathematical equations as they were originally written.

For example, to write the equation $A = B + C$, the programmer would write the following in short code:

$$00 \ S0 \ 03 \ S1 \ 07 \ S2$$

S0, S1, and S2 stand for the quantities A, B, and C respectively, and

03 and 07 stand for the equal sign and the addition sign respectively. The 00 designates the line number of the operation.

Grace's years of experience working with computers and writing programs made her believe that a computer could be used to write its own programs. She reasoned that the computer, this huge and powerful machine, would do the work. She recognized too that the big obstacle holding back the spread of computers to nonscientific and business use was that few people could write the code or program for the new machines. The early computers were far from user friendly.

Grace Hopper knew the key to opening up the world of computers to broader nonscientific and business use was in the further development and refinement of programming languages. Languages were needed that could be understood and used by people who were not mathematicians or computer experts.

One of the first steps to confirm the belief that computers could write programs was the development of a program by Frances E. (Betty) Holberton called "Sort-Merge Generator." A sort-merge program sorts files of data and arranges them in some desired order, such as by date or code number. Betty worked for the National Bureau of Standards. With this program, she demonstrated that she could generate sort/merge routines. (Grace Hopper recalls that it was Betty who taught her how to write flowcharts for computer programs.)

In 1950 the Eckert-Mauchly Corporation was bought by Remington Rand, and in 1955 Remington Rand was merged into the Sperry Corporation. Grace Hopper stayed on through all of these changes until her retirement from Sperry in 1971. The Sperry Corporation later became known as UNISYS.

By sometime in the middle of 1952, Grace Hopper flatly made the statement, "I could make a computer do anything which I could completely define."

In that year she completed her first compiler, known as the A-0

System (the A stands for algebraic) at Remington Rand. The A-0 System was a set of instructions that could translate symbolic mathematical code into machine code that the computer could understand and use to perform a calculation.

Grace Hopper put the pieces of code or programming routines she had collected over the years on magnetic tape. The programming routines all started at "0" (zero), but to go into a program in the proper sequence or order, they had to have call numbers added to them. At UNIVAC, Grace gave each routine a call number. Then if she needed subroutines for a program she was writing, she did not need to copy them in machine language. "All I had to do was to

Years later, Grace Hopper was honored for her work in developing computer programs. Here she receives the American Federation of Information Processing Societies' Harry Goode Memorial Award in 1970.

write down a set of call numbers, let the computer find them on the tape, bring them over and do the additions. This was the first compiler," she declared.

Grace quickly realized that "We could start writing mathematical equations and let the computer do the work. The computer would call the pieces and put them together."

These innovations were a revelation. When Grace first started programming computers, all the programs had to be written in machine language or code. The repetitive writing of numbers led to frequent mistakes in the programming. It was in an effort to try to overcome some of this difficulty and to make the programs error-free that Grace continued to work at improving computer languages.

Grace Hopper describes how she solved a problem that came up when she was developing the A-0 compiler. The problem existed whenever she had to jump forward in the program to a section that had not yet been written.

As an undergraduate at college, Grace played basketball under the women's rules in effect at that time. There were six players on a team and the court was divided into two halves. Each team had both a center and a side center. Grace was the side center on her team.

The old rules specified that you could dribble only once and you couldn't take a step while the ball was in your hands. In order to get under the basket, you had to make what was called a "forward pass." You threw the ball to another member of your team, ran "like the dickens" up ahead, and then she threw the ball back to you.

Grace thought she could adapt this concept to solve the problem of forward jumps in a computer program. She says, "I tucked a little section down at the end of the memory which I called the 'neutral corner.' At the time I wanted to jump forward from the routine I was working on, I jumped to a spot in the 'neutral corner.' I then set up a flag for an operation which said, 'I've got a message for you.'

This meant that each routine, as I processed it, had to look and see if it had a flag; if it did, it put a second jump from the neutral corner to the beginning of the routine, and it was possible to make a single-pass compiler—and the concept did come from playing basketball!"

In 1952, Grace wrote a paper on compilers, the first of over fifty papers she has had published on programming languages and computer software. As recently as 1984, she coauthored a book, *Understanding Computers*, and a reprint of her article, "The Education of a Computer," was published in the *Annals of the History of Computing*, Volume 9, Number 3/4, 1988. Grace's 1952 paper on compilers led to her appointment as Systems Engineer, Director of Automatic Programming Development for Remington Rand. This was another good "forward pass" completed to advance Grace's career.

12

Leading the Way With Flowmatic

After the A-0 System compiler came improved versions, A-1 and A-2. A-2 was completed by Grace Hopper and her staff in 1955 and was the first compiler to be used extensively. This series of compilers broke ground and helped to lead the way toward the development of programming languages. Some of the first steps taken before A-0 included the library of programs for the Mark I developed under Howard Aiken and the development of sets of mathematical subroutines for a British computer called EDSAC, or Electronic Delay Storage Automatic Computer.

The development of EDSAC gave another clue to the possible interest businesses might have in using computers. The Lyons Tea Company of England approached Maurice Wilkes, who was building EDSAC, to ask if they could contribute to the cost of constructing EDSAC. Then if it was a success, they would go ahead and design and build a computer for use by the tea company. Results with EDSAC were encouraging, so LEO, or the Lyons Electronic Office, was built.

Meanwhile in the United States, Eckert-Mauchly signed a contract to deliver the UNIVAC I, one of the first general purpose, electronic, stored-program computers, to the A. C. Nielsen Company for use in taking surveys. Only an hour after the polls had closed for the national election in 1952 and with only 7 percent of the votes counted, the UNIVAC I predicted the landslide vote for Dwight Eisenhower. The vote was so lopsided, however, that the results were not released right away. Everyone thought the computer had made a mistake!

Also in the early 1950s IBM started to build production model scientific computers. The first was called the 701. Production of a business version of the 701, the 702, was started as well.

Still, the key to success in widening the use of computers was programming language development. In 1954, IBM made a commitment to develop an automatic programming language. The outcome was a scientific programming language known as FORTRAN, short for FORmula TRANslation. FORTRAN was designed to be used on the IBM 704 and is one of the leading scientific programming languages. Nevertheless, FORTRAN and the IBM 704 computer were useful only to scientists and did not help businesses to use computers to process information.

The A-0 System compiler changed mathematical notations into machine language or code that the computer could understand. Not long after Grace completed the first compiler, she gave a talk on it. The usual response was, "You can't do that." Grace said that it took two years before others began to accept the idea. "I had a running compiler," she said, "and nobody would touch it because, they carefully told me, computers could only do arithmetic; they could not do programs. It was a selling job to get people to try it. I think with any new idea, because people are allergic to change, you have to get out and sell the idea."

A key idea Grace Hopper originated is that computer programs could be written in English. She viewed each of the letters of the alphabet as simply another kind of symbol just like mathematical symbols. The computer could be made to translate the letters of the alphabet into machine code. This idea was unheard of at the time, but it was the beginning of an important computer language for businesses that Grace Hopper helped to develop.

"No one thought of that earlier," Dr. Hopper says, "because they weren't as lazy as I was. A lot of our programmers like to play with the bits. I wanted to get jobs done. That's what the computer was there for."

Though everybody turned down Grace Hopper's idea that computer programs could be written in English, she followed her own philosophy of "go ahead and do it. You can always apologize later." She moved forward and developed the B-0 compiler (B stands for business), which later became known as Flowmatic. She worked at

Dr. Hopper working on a program for UNIVAC.

creating a language that businesses could use for tasks such as automatic billing and calculating payroll. By the end of 1956, UNIVAC I and II were "understanding" twenty statements in English.

Now Dr. Hopper realized that money was needed to continue to work on Flowmatic. She and her staff would have to go before a budget committee and prove the worth of what they were doing in order to get more funds. They decided to give a special demonstration for the budget committee. Not only would they make a pilot model English language program, they would also change words in the compiler to make a French and a German program!

Alas, the idea did not go over well with the members of the budget committee. She and her team were told that an American computer built in Philadelphia, Pennsylvania, couldn't understand French or German! It took four months before Grace and her staff could sufficiently smooth over their efforts to get a budget for expanding Flowmatic.

Flowmatic was an enormous advance in the development of programming languages for computers. It was the first computer program to introduce understandable English words for both the data to be operated upon and the instructions for the operation or calculation. Typical commands used included words such as COUNT, DIVIDE, SUBTRACT, MOVE, REPLACE, and MULTIPLY. Anyone could recognize the meaning of these commands.

By 1957, three major computer languages were being used in American computers. These were known as APT (Automatically Programmed Tools), IBM's FORTRAN, and Grace Hopper's Flowmatic. The three languages were entirely different from one another. They could be used on only one specific computer, and Flowmatic was the only language that used English commands.

Other competing computer languages were also being developed, however. There soon was a need to devise a universal computer language or risk ending up with a modern-day Tower of

Babel, a confusion of many languages. (The building of the Tower of Babel, as described in the Bible in the Book of Genesis, was interrupted by a confusion of many tongues or languages.) Ideally, a universal computer language would be usable on any machine and could be understood by people other than mathematicians and computer experts.

UNIVAC managers said what business customers wanted was a way to process the data or information necessary to efficiently run their companies. "Dealing with data ushered in a whole new world," Grace Hopper recalls. "We lost all our checking ability. We lost our language in mathematics—a well-known, universal language, as easily understood here as in Tokyo or Berlin. We were dealing suddenly with words."

In response, Grace Hopper wrote 500 typical programs and identified thirty verbs that she thought would be common to all of the programs. But when she recommended that data processing programs be written in English, she recalls, "I was told very quickly that I couldn't do this because computers didn't understand English." Three years passed before her idea was accepted as workable.

13

The Race to Develop COBOL

The growing need for a universal computer programming language led to an important discussion between Mary Hawes of the Burroughs Company and Dr. Saul Gorn of the University of Pennsylvania at the Western Joint Computer Conference in San Francisco in early March 1959. They agreed then that a common business language was necessary.

On April 8, 1959, a meeting was held to talk about the leadership needed to develop a common business language. Grace Hopper was there. She suggested that Charles Phillips of the Department of Defense would be an excellent choice to head up such an effort. He would be able to supply energetic leadership and yet would be neutral about proposals for the language since he was not associated directly with any commercial company. An added advantage was that he had the stature and the access to a budget that would command the respect of manufacturers.

At this same meeting Phillips was made head of an executive committee to steer the project. The committee consisted of representative Joe Cunningham from the Air Force as vice chairman, Gene Albertson of United States Steel, Greg Dillon of Du Pont, Mel

Grosz of Standard Oil Company (ESSO), and the chairmen of three task groups that had been established.

The task groups were known as Short Range, Intermediate Range, and Long Range groups. The Short Range task group, headed by Joe Wegstein, was given three months to come up with a composite language derived from the best features of the three most common languages in use.

Many did not believe the task group could accomplish the job in so little time, but the group held a dozen meetings between June 23 and the end of August. Those who participated were from the Burroughs Company, International Business Machines, Minneapolis Honeywell, Radio Corporation of America, Remington Rand UNIVAC, and Sylvania. Representatives of the Air Materiel Command and the Bureau of Ships also were there.

Despite the many meetings held by the task group, the report presented to the executive committee on September 4 was a hodgepodge. The task group had not been able to reach agreement among themselves. The group was urgently told to get the composite in shape by December 1.

Meanwhile, a new company was being formed, Computer Sciences Corporation. It was developing a compiler for the Honeywell 800 computer. Joe Wegstein told the executive committee the details of this development on September 4, when the Short Range task group's unacceptable report was made.

On October 8, one of the members of the Intermediate Range task group, Dr. Richard Clippinger of Honeywell, was able to show the committee a copy of the Honeywell Business Compiler Language that later became known as FACT. FACT brought together several of the features that had been tried during the development of IBM's Commercial Translator language. Influenced by the unorganized presentation of the Short Range task group, the Intermediate Range group immediately endorsed FACT to be the basis for the common business language.

This one-upmanship caused shock waves at IBM and UNIVAC. These companies had agreed to work toward a composite common business language. Now they were being asked to accept in entirety the language of a competitor. The race to develop a common business language became all the more feverish.

Later when it came time to demonstrate FACT, the language could not be made to run successfully in actual practice.

The Short Range task group gave its next report in January 1960. This time it was accepted. It was edited by Phillips, Wegstein, and Betty Holberton. This process took until April. Finally, the Government Printing Office issued the COBOL 60 Report in June. COBOL is shorthand for COmmon Business Oriented Language. (See additional information about COBOL at the back of this book.)

Though the COBOL 60 Report had shortcomings, the list of manufacturers who announced that they would use the COBOL language grew. However, for general acceptance in industry, it was critical that IBM also accept the COBOL language.

At first, IBM wanted to continue with two languages. It had developed Commercial Translator and also wanted to use COBOL. This was not acceptable to the members of the Conference on Data Systems Languages (CODASYL) as the steering committee was now titled. Its members had expanded to include eleven manufacturers: the original six of the Short Range task group (Burroughs, International Business Machines, Minneapolis Honeywell, Radio Corporation of America, Remington Rand UNIVAC, and Sylvania) plus Bendix, Computer Sciences Corporation, General Electric, National Cash Register, and Philco.

During the year 1960 many companies announced that they would develop COBOL compilers.

In an article on the front page of the business section of *The New York Times* dated August 26, 1960, RCA had claimed victory in the "Computer Translating Race." The article continued, "COBOL, for Common Business Oriented Language, substitutes simple English key words for present complicated numerical jargon understood only by electronic computer specialists to 'instruct' a computer in its functions."

Within the same news copy, Dr. Grace Murray Hopper, chief engineer for automatic programming for the Sperry Corporation's Remington Rand Division, declared: "We shall definitely have a COBOL programming system available on our UNIVAC II computer by October 31."

"Remington Rand had been Radio Corporation's closest rival in the COBOL programming race," stated the article.

On December 6, 1960, UNIVAC and RCA introduced to the public their version of COBOL. They demonstrated before the news media that the common business oriented language they had developed could be run on two different computers. Charles Phillips from the Department of Defense and R. W. Bremer of IBM were present. And as always, at the leading edge of what was going on, Dr. Grace Murray Hopper took part in the demonstration.

The two computers operated the test COBOL programs identically. On December 6, UNIVAC II ran the program and on December 7, the RCA 501 computer ran the same program to demonstrate that the COBOL program was compatible with either computer.

As one of the companies involved in the COBOL race, IBM also had received newspaper publicity about its progress in the development of computer programming languages. But the company did not feel that COBOL was ready to use as a substitute for numerical computer programming as early as other companies in the competition. Not until September 1962 did IBM spokesman Bob Ruthrauff declare, "We intend to make COBOL our development language and plan no further development of the Commercial Translator language itself." This was the IBM acceptance of the COBOL language that had been sought since 1960.

Evaluation by the United States Navy showed that techniques

Dr. Grace M. Hopper testing COBOL.

of early COBOL programs were very primitive. There was a great range in the cost of using the programs, and the rate at which the program would run varied drastically with the size of the memory available on the computer being used.

The European Computer Manufacturers Association (ECMA) set up a Technical Committee to deal with COBOL. It corresponded to the American National Standards Institute's X3.4.4 committee, which now was responsible for standardizing the COBOL programming language. The two committees worked together to publish a dozen information bulletins about COBOL.

Among the publications were COBOL 60, COBOL 61, COBOL

Dr. Hopper teaching others about COBOL.

61 Extended, COBOL 65, CODASYL COBOL Journal of Development-69, and CODASYL COBOL Journal of Development-70. Originally, there was to be a yearly update as the COBOL programming language was developed.

Today COBOL is one of the most widely used computer languages in the world. There are many reasons. COBOL is the computer language that the United States Defense Department urged United States businesses to adopt. Many businesses did so in order to continue selling their products to the government. COBOL also is designed to be used on almost any business computer.

Another very important feature of COBOL is that it uses English-like sentences that make it easier to understand. In addition, COBOL is very efficient at processing large quantities of information for businesses, and the language is continually being updated and improved.

Dr. Hopper is considered one of the primary leaders in standardizing computer languages. She was at the first meetings of the Committee on Data Systems Languages (CODASYL) and served on the American National Standards Institute's X3.4 committee. Betty Holberton, who worked for the National Bureau of Standards and who also helped forge the development of programming languages, credits Grace Hopper with speaking to management "in terms they could understand." Holberton says that was Grace's "real strength."

14

A Brief Retirement

Grace Murray Hopper had been a consultant and lecturer for the United States Naval Reserve since 1946, in addition to her work at civilian jobs. In 1966 she received a letter from the Chief of Naval Personnel. It pointed out that she had been on reserve duty for twenty-three years, which was more than twenty. "I knew that," Grace said. Another paragraph stated she was sixty years old. "I knew that too," she said. "The next paragraph stated, 'Please apply for retirement.' So, I did." On December 31, 1966, the Navy placed Grace Hopper on the Naval Reserve retired list with the rank of commander. "It was the saddest day of my life," said Grace.

This retirement was to last a mere seven months.

United States Public Law 89-306, known as the Brooks Bill, makes the setting of standards for federal information processing the responsibility of the National Bureau of Standards (NBS), the Office of Management and Budget (formerly the Bureau of the Budget), and the General Services Administration.

The first man in the National Bureau of Standards to be charged with the responsibility to oversee the standardization of COBOL language was Norman Ream. He had previously been Special

Assistant to the Secretary of the Navy for Automatic Data Processing. While Ream was special assistant, he had called upon Grace Murray Hopper to solve a difficult problem.

At that time, many compilers claimed to be COBOL, but the user of the program often was misled. One version of COBOL might run on a particular computer and another version might not. Ream wanted Grace Hopper to standardize COBOL for the Navy.

As Grace put it, "I came running—I always do when the Navy sends for me." Accordingly Grace Hopper returned to temporary active duty on August 1, 1967. Her job was to lead a concentrated effort to standardize COBOL for the Navy and to persuade the entire Navy to use this high-level computer language.

Grace Hopper was installed in an office in the Pentagon and provided with a small staff. Supplies were meager, and there was no computer. After buying a coffeepot to get things rolling, Grace and her staff furnished the entire office within a couple of weeks. She followed some advice a chief had given her long ago: "If you need something, 'liberate,' or borrow, it from the Air Force—they have everything; if you can't find it there, get it from the Army—they have almost everything and they don't know how to count; but there is no use trying to 'liberate' it from the Seabees or Marines because they liberated it to begin with." There was good reason for a Jolly Roger flag hoisted above Grace Hopper's desk—she earned the right to fly the pirate's skull and crossbones!

Initially, Grace was asked to return to active duty for six months, but soon her orders read "indefinite" when referring to how long her services would be needed. Under her direction, the Navy was able to develop a COBOL certifier that was available to anyone. The certifier was a set of programs that would tell the user whether a compiler labeled COBOL met the standards of the COBOL language and could be used on any COBOL compatible computer.

While Grace Hopper served as Director, Navy Programming Languages Group, Office of Information Systems Planning and

Development, she and her staff prepared helpful materials for the use of COBOL. For example, a translator was developed to convert COBOL '61, '62, and '65 statements into USA Standard COBOL statements. The translator also could detect unfamiliar, nonstandard statements in the older versions of COBOL.

A preprocessor was developed that consisted of either a set of routines for use on smaller computers or a routine with many options for use on larger computers.

A Navy manual, *Fundamentals of COBOL*, was published to train people to use COBOL. In addition, a catalog was produced with an index of sample statements that illustrated how to use

Former First Lady Mamie Eisenhower congratulates Commander Hopper after she was presented with the Science Achievement Award by the American Mothers Committee.

Standard COBOL. Helpful hints also were collected as experience in the use of COBOL accumulated. Guides for instructors and students were produced.

Grace Hopper still thinks that standards for computer languages have not been strict enough, however. "By not adopting—or following—standards, the federal government spends $450 million a year converting computer programs," she reasons. "A real waste of money."

The "indefinite" term of Grace Hopper's stay in the United States Navy lasted nearly twenty years. As Grace puts it, "so far, it has been the longest six months I've ever spent."

Soon after she had devised the COBOL certifier for the Navy, she was invited to give a presentation to the Secretary of the Navy and other officials of high rank. She practiced her presentation over and over again for weeks.

As she walked to the meeting accompanied by a Navy captain, he said, "This is the first time a woman has ever given a presentation in that room." She says of the Navy captain's remark, "He said that so I would feel more at ease."

A little nearer the room, the captain said, "This is the first time anyone below the rank of captain has given a presentation in that room." At that time Grace held the rank of commander. "I was in fine shape by the time I got there," she recalls.

After her presentation, the Secretary of the Navy asked Commander Hopper if there was anything he could do to help. Unfazed by the high-ranking audience, Grace did not hesitate to reply. She said she could use a larger staff and an additional twenty thousand dollars to conduct a survey on the needs of COBOL users. The Secretary promised he would do whatever he could about the request. Then Grace remembers that "the room collapsed in one roar of laughter."

Leaving quickly to seek the comfort of the hallway outside the room, Commander Hopper asked the Navy captain, "What have I done this time?" He answered, "Don't you realize that no one ever asks for less than twenty million dollars in that room?"

In 1973, President Richard M. Nixon promoted Commander Grace Murray Hopper to captain.

In addition to her work for the Navy and private industry, Grace Hopper has never lost her love of teaching others. She has been associated with the Moore School of Electrical Engineering of the University of Pennsylvania, where she had been a visiting lecturer in 1959 and in 1962 a visiting assistant professor. In 1963 she became visiting associate professor and in 1973 an adjunct professor of engineering. Also in 1971, she was made professorial lecturer in management science at George Washington University in Washington, D.C.

15

Grace Hopper, Tireless Teacher to Us All

For many years now Grace Murray Hopper has spent much of her time as a tireless and inspiring speaker to many different kinds of audiences. She is a powerhouse who is comfortable talking about her youth, about the years she and others have spent developing modern computers and computer languages, or about what the future holds for computers, people, and this country.

Whenever Grace Hopper gave a speech while still in the Naval Reserve, she usually wore her uniform and her cap as an "identifier." She pointed out to her audience that every record in a computer has to have an identifier in order to store it and to be able to retrieve it at a later time.

Grace has often told humorous stories about wandering around airports in her Navy uniform and having people come up to her and say, "When's the next plane for Houston?" She said, "I got totally demoted one night in San Francisco. I got off an elevator and I heard a woman say to her husband,'What was that?' And he said, 'That was a security guard.'"

Continued Grace, "So then I went up to Canada to speak at the University of Guelph, and I had to go through Immigration at the

Toronto Airport. I handed my passport to the Immigration officer, and he looked at it and looked at me and said, 'What are you?' And I said, 'United States Navy.' He took a second real hard look at me, and then he said, 'You must be the oldest one they've got.'" Grace Hopper didn't think that was a very pleasant way to be welcomed to Canada.

In some of her speeches, Grace Hopper compared the computers of today to early automobiles. "I've never forgotten how they [cars] changed the world of transportation," she remarked. Grace can remember when Riverside Drive along the Hudson River in New York City was a dirt road. On Sunday afternoons families would go outside and sit on the drive and watch all the beautiful horses and carriages go by. "All afternoon there might be one car," said Grace.

"Cars were enormously expensive," she added. "They were individually built. There were no such things as gas stations. When you went on a long trip, you got five gallon cans of gasoline, put 'em on the back decks, strapped them to the car, and took them with you. If you broke down in the middle of Utah, you wired back to the manufacturer and he sent a man with a part. Then he worked on the part until it fitted your car," Grace explained.

Grace recalls that when more people began owning cars, gas stations appeared, garages stocked the interchangeable parts, roads were demanded, and transportation totally changed.

"Along came a gentleman named Henry Ford with two concepts: standard interchangeable parts and an assembly line," Grace continued. He started to built Model T's. "You could have any color as long as it was black, and the cost was between $300 and $600," said Grace. Folks began to own cars. Everybody began to buy cars, and the whole world changed as a result.

Adding to these comments, Dr. Hopper has said, "I think we failed to recognize that today we have the Model T in the computer industry. People are beginning to own them [computers], and we

Captain Hopper at work in her office in August 1976.

are now at the very beginning of what will be the largest industry in the United States."

Continuing with her analogy to transportation, Grace Hopper has warned against making the same kind of mistake we did with transportation. "We got so fascinated with those cars that we totally neglected the railroads—we did not look at transportation as a whole, and because we didn't, the railroads are falling apart. The truth of the matter is that we've done a lousy job of managing transportation as a whole."

Grace believes that the computer industry will not make the same mistakes so long as it realizes that any effort to computerize a company should look at the total flow of information within that company. A business should also place a value on its information. Dr. Hopper says we must recognize that some information is good overnight, and some is good for a thousand years.

To stress the importance of placing a value on information, Grace Hopper has sometimes described in her speeches an imaginary chemical plant where all the operations are computerized. She has asked her audience to suppose that at 10:00 A.M. two messages come in. One tells you that a valve inside the plant is not functioning properly, and if it is not repaired within ten minutes, the whole plant will blow up; the other message tells you that an employee worked two hours overtime last week. Which message is more important?

Information also should be as complete as possible. An example Grace Hopper has cited is that of the captain of a ship who asks how many gallons of fuel remain. "Do you just tell him how many gallons there are?" she asks. "No, that would be an insufficient answer." Think how much more useful it would be to tell him that he has seventy gallons, that he is steaming northwest into a northwest wind, and that he can continue to do this for a certain number of hours. This is a full and relative answer.

Another consideration is accuracy of information. If the information given to a computer from files is not correct in the first place, then the computer's solutions to problems also will not be correct. Such mistakes can be extremely costly.

Often in Dr. Hopper's speeches she has related the following story. A young Navy officer wanted to keep his maintenance records for his carrier-based airplane during a tour at sea. He made friends with the land-based programmer who had the necessary records. He copied the records and stored them in his personal computer, which he then stowed behind the seat of the plane. After his tour, he mentioned how successful his plan had been. It was then that someone questioned, "Were you supposed to do that?" The officer replied, "I didn't ask."

Dr. Hopper has enjoyed telling this tale because it leads her to one of her most important pieces of advice for all of us. "When you have a good idea and you've tried it and you know it's going to work, go ahead and do it—because it is much easier to apologize later than it is to get permission."

As the computers Grace worked with became faster and faster, she found it more and more difficult to comprehend the units of time that they operated in. She asked herself, "What is a millisecond?" She knew the definition of a millisecond was one-thousandth of a second. However, she said, "I could see a second, but darned if I could see a thousandth of it." And now computers were developed that measured time in microseconds (one-millionth of a second), nanoseconds (one-billionth of a second), and picoseconds (one-trillionth of a second).

One day in total frustration, Grace called the engineering building and said, "Please cut off a nanosecond and send it over to me." What she received was a piece of wire that represented the maximum distance electricity could travel in the wire in one-billionth of a second. (This also is the distance that light can travel in space in one-billionth of a second.) A piece of wire that represents a nanosecond is 11.78 inches long.

Grace Hopper liked her nanosecond so much that she asked for something to compare it to. The next "piece" of wire she received represented a microsecond—it was a coil of wire 984 feet long. She says, "Sometimes I think that we should hang one on all programmers' desks or around their necks so they know exactly what they are throwing away when they throw away a microsecond."

As for picoseconds, Dr. Hopper has told her audiences they can be found wrapped in small paper packets at fast-food restaurants. The packets are labeled "pepper," but the black specs inside are really picoseconds!

Another anecdote Grace has told is the story of an admiral who wanted to know why it took so long to send a message by satellite. "I had to point out to him that between here and the satellite, there were a very large number of nanoseconds," she quipped, as she demonstrated by pointing a nanosecond-long piece of wire toward space.

In the over two hundred lectures given each year by Grace Hopper, she discusses the future of computers and important ways in which they will be used.

One thing she thinks will happen is that the home computer industry will grow larger and larger as the price of personal computers shrinks. Grace Hopper envisions the day when home computer systems will be so common that they will be used to control our home environment. Heating, air conditioning, lights, and security systems will be controlled by computer with a great savings in the use of energy resources.

Computers will be useful for many other applications, including family bookkeeping, money management, and even sports and hobbies. Grace knows one fisherman who keeps complete computer records of all of the fish he catches. He records, for example, their size and weight, where caught, lure used, and weather conditions. She herself would like to keep all of her knitting instructions on file in a computer. Then she would not have to go hunting in the back room for the directions to knit the beautiful sweaters and other items she makes for her many grandnephews and grandnieces.

Systems of computers to do certain jobs are what Dr. Hopper talks about in her recent speeches. Centralized processors will no longer be considered fast enough. Again, as the price of computers drops, many businesses that earlier could afford only one centralized computer now will be able to afford several computers operating in parallel as a network.

Grace tells a story to illustrate this point. In the old days farmers used an ox to pull a heavy log out of the woods after felling a tree. When one ox was not able to budge the load, the farmers did not try to grow a bigger ox. Instead they used two oxen. Well, it's the same with computers. When one computer is not enough to do a job, "Don't get a bigger computer—get another computer," advises Dr. Hopper.

One other idea Grace Hopper says has been around for years but that hasn't been used adequately yet is specialized computers that are designed for a specific job. An application Dr. Hopper cites is for artificial intelligence (AI). She says that AI is not going to move ahead until its data base (stored information a computer can call on to help it solve a problem) is much bigger.

Sometimes people ask Dr. Hopper why increased speed in computers is important. Right off the bat, she mentions two tremendous problems that are of consequence to life on Earth. One is to improve weather forecasting on a long-range global scale to produce larger food crops. Another is managing the earth's water supplies in a fair and equitable manner.

As the world population continues to grow, we must increase food supplies. In order to do this, we must have better weather forecasting. "Yet we do not today have a computer that will run a full-scale model of the big heat engine which consists of the atmosphere and the ocean," states Dr. Hopper. She goes on to say that until a few years ago we didn't even have enough data to feed to the faster computers. But now satellite photographs are so good that "when fully enhanced by computer, you can tell how high the waves are out in the middle of the Pacific and tell what the temperature of the ocean is twenty feet below the surface."

"Of course there's a catch. To fully enhance a satellite photograph takes 10 to the fifteenth power arithmetic operations. That's 10 with fifteen zeros after it. That's about three days on our best computers and the weather has already happened. Yet we must have that weather information. It's critical," Grace warns.

The other enormous problem Grace Hopper foresees is being

↑ 19:31 19DE88 19A-Z 0090-1640 ED1   ↓

A computerized weather satellite photograph showing cloud patterns on December 19, 1988.

studied by the Army Corps of Engineers and other government agencies. She cites several places in the United States where water is already in short supply. One is in the state of Colorado, where the eastern half of the state is dry and the western half has enough water. The people in the eastern half of the state want the westerners to share their water supply, but the westerners say, "No way." In addition, in Florida so much water has been drawn out of the underlying aquifer that sinkholes large enough to engulf whole houses and cars have appeared. The entire city of Tucson, Arizona, is sinking for the same reason.

Many cities in the United States have had to limit the use of water by individuals in order to have enough to distribute to everyone. In New Jersey, where Grace Hopper's sister lives, water was limited to fifty gallons per day per person one recent summer. Grace says that eventually we're going to have to manage all of the water supplies in the United States to insure that each person gets a fair share, and the problem is much closer than we may think.

At the twenty-fifth anniversary dinner of the invention of the computer, held in Chicago in August 1971, Grace told of a goal she has had since childhood. She had always wanted to get to the stars. She explained, "Some day many millions of years from now the sun will go nova—that is blow up, and the universe with it. We must get off the planet Earth and find another place for the human race to live. The present is not too soon to start on this quest. The computer will be man's greatest tool in attaining this new home for mankind."

Because of the importance of computers in our future, schools need to teach computer literacy to all their students. But first the teachers, "who for the most part are scared of computers," says Dr. Hopper, must become comfortable with the technology. Not only teachers, but most people are afraid of change, Grace feels. But she remembers when people would not touch telephones for fear of being electrocuted. She also says people took a while to adapt to the electric refrigerator. Many people thought the only way you could keep lettuce fresh was on ice, and so they thought they needed an icebox for that purpose.

Dr. Hopper says we spend too much time talking about hardware and software and not enough time discussing the information we want to computerize and the people who will work with the computers.

Grace Hopper wants to live to be ninety-four. She says, "I have two reasons. The first is that the party on December 31, 1999, will be a New Year's Eve party to end all New Year's Eve parties. The second is that I want to point back to the early days of the computer and say to all the doubters, 'See? We told you the computer could do all that!'"

The future is always on Grace Hopper's mind. She becomes particularly enthusiastic when she talks about future computers. "Within five years you're going to have computers driven by light," she predicts. But she wonders how to tell an admiral that instead of sending messages in bleeps and blips of sound or electricity over copper wires, you are now going to send them in photons or small bursts of light energy over hair-thin glass optical fibers.

Changing someone's mind, says Grace, "is the toughest job there is. With any new idea, you have to sell that idea and market it. In the long run, you don't do it by logic. You've got to show that guy why it's in his interest to accept a new way."

16

Well Done, Admiral

Among the many awards Grace Hopper has received, she says the first one means the most to her. This was the Naval Ordnance Development Award presented to her in 1946. She compares it to a pat on the back that says, "You're on the right track. Keep up the good work."

The first person ever to receive the Computer Science Man-of-the-Year Award from the Data Processing Management Association was Grace Hopper in 1969. Each year the award is given to recognize internationally an individual who has made an outstanding contribution to the field of computer science.

In 1971, the UNIVAC division of Sperry Corporation initiated the Grace Murray Hopper Award to be given annually to "honor a young computer professional—male or female—adjudged to have made a significant contribution to computer science." The first award was made in August 1971, at the Association for Computing Machinery Conference that celebrated the twenty-fifth anniversary of the public unveiling of ENIAC.

In May 1973, Grace Hopper was awarded the Legion of Merit. This honor, derived from the Badge for Military Merit instituted in

1782 by George Washington, was created by Congress in 1942. It is granted to enlisted military personnel from the United States and other countries friendly to the United States for the performance of outstanding services.

While Grace Hopper was head of the Programming Language Section of the Naval Information Systems Division, she was presented a certificate of promotion to the rank of captain. The ceremony took place in the Pentagon office of Admiral Elmo R. Zumwalt, Jr., on August 13, 1973.

Also in 1973, Grace Hopper became the first woman and the first person from the United States to be made a Distinguished Fellow of the British Computer Society. She traveled to London to receive the award.

As Grace describes it, there is nothing more formal than a formal dinner in London. When she arrived at the dinner in her full-length dress Navy uniform and tiara, she was informed that her escort for the evening would be Lord Mountbatten. Grace confesses that she was scared. "I didn't know what to do with royalty and lords . . . . But he was charming, utterly charming."

At dinner, she had in her purse one of the very first computer chips. "He was fascinated by it," says Grace. Lord Mountbatten gave her the cues for when to get up, when to sit down, and when to toast the Queen.

When Grace rose to accept the honor, she was uncertain if she should use her usual speech closing in England, but she decided to stick to her guns. So she thanked them for the honor and said she was grateful to receive it, but had to remind them, "I have already received the highest award, which is the honor and privilege of serving very proudly in the United States Navy."

As Grace turned to sit down, Lord Mountbatten said, "Well done, Captain." Grace knew that he was a Navy man.

In 1968 she was given the Connelly Memorial Award of the Miami Valley Computer Association, in 1970 the Science Achieve-

Admiral Elmo R. Zumwalt, Jr., Chief of Naval Operations, promotes Commander Hopper to the rank of captain, August 13, 1973.

ment Award of the American Mothers Committee and the American Federation of Information Processing Societies' Harry Goode Memorial Award. In 1972 Grace Hopper received the Wilbur L. Cross Medal from Yale University, in 1980 the United States Navy's Meritorious Service Medal, in 1983 the Pioneer Medal of the Institute of Electrical and Electronic Engineers Computer Society and the American Association of University Women Achievement Award, and in 1984 the Woman of the Year Award of the Young Women's Christian Association of the National Capitol Area. These are just a few examples of recognition given to Dr. Hopper.

Wolfeboro, New Hampshire, where she spent her summers as a youth, is a second home for Grace Murray Hopper. Her brother, Roger F. Murray II, currently lives in Wolfeboro year round. The town has a small private school, Brewster Academy, situated on the shore of Lake Winnipesaukee. In November 1982, Captain Grace Murray Hopper came to the school to speak to the students.

Before she arrived, some of the students seemed somewhat skeptical. After all, what could a little old white-haired lady say to them about computers? But as soon as she began to speak on the day of her visit, Grace Hopper held the students' rapt attention. The speech turned into an hour-and-a-half sharing of ideas and went on to include her appearance at two COBOL programming classes.

When Captain Hopper suggested that she might be able to get additional support for Brewster's efforts to teach computer programming, the idea to establish a computer center at the school was born.

Captain Hopper and the staff of Brewster Academy worked and kept in touch with each other through the school year. When the center was ready to open, she personally invited Dr. An Wang, founder of Wang Laboratories, and Dr. Kenneth Olsen, president of the Digital Equipment Corporation, to the dedication. In the end, the ceremonies to dedicate the new computer center were attended by representatives of about one hundred and fifty corporations.

When Kenneth Olsen arrived by helicopter, he brought a surprise for the school from the Digital Equipment Corporation, a gift of two DECmate II word processors and a printer for the new computer center.

Also present at the festivities as President Reagan's personal emissary was Rear Admiral Paul E. Sutherland, Jr., Commander of the Naval Data Automation Command in Washington, D.C. Richard Bloch and Robert Campbell, Hopper's fellow programmers years ago on the Mark I, were there as well.

On November 7, 1983, approximately one year after the idea for a computer center was put forth, the Grace Murray Hopper

Captain Hopper with Brewster Academy students, November 7, 1983.

Center for Computer Learning was opened at Brewster Academy. A bronze plaque was unveiled at the ceremonies.

That same day, Governor John Sununu of New Hampshire issued a proclamation declaring November 7, 1983, "Captain Grace Murray Hopper Day" throughout the state. Meanwhile, also on that day, though technically too old to be promoted, Grace Hopper was made a commodore by a special act of Congress.

Later, on December 15, 1983, Grace Hopper and several members of her family attended the formal ceremony at the White House in Washington, D.C. Secretary of the Navy John Lehman promoted Captain Hopper to the rank of commodore as President Ronald Reagan looked on. Then President Reagan congratulated Commodore Hopper and shook hands with her.

Approximately a year after becoming a commodore, on November 15, 1984, Grace Murray Hopper was inducted into the Engineering and Science Hall of Fame. The citation stated:

> In tribute to your superior technical competence and mathematical genius; in tribute to your creative leadership, vision, and commitment as a computer pioneer; in tribute to your setting a foremost example as an author and inventor; in tribute to your dedication to the human and humane elements of teaching, learning, and scholarship; and in tribute to your insights and innovations in meeting the challenges of rapidly changing times, we induct you—Commodore Grace Murray Hopper—into the Engineering and Science Hall of Fame.

The ceremony took place in Dayton, Ohio. Two other individuals who were inducted with Grace Hopper that day were George Washington Carver and Henry Heimlich.

George Washington Carver (1864-1943) was born to parents who were slaves. Later, he became best remembered for his contributions in agriculture, which included research on peanuts and sweet potatoes. These crops enriched the soil where they were

Commodore Hopper (center) stands with President Ronald Reagan and members of her family after her promotion at the White House. From left to right, her family members are nephew Roger Murray III, his daughter Jennifer, and his wife Linda.

planted and thus helped southern farmers to revitalize their land after years of planting soil-exhausting cotton.

In 1974, Henry Heimlich (1920-) devised a method to rescue a choking person that became known as the Heimlich Maneuver. His method was so successful that he is credited with saving the lives of more Americans than anyone now living.

Among the previous six inductees to the Engineering and Science Hall of Fame were Jonas Salk, whose research produced the Salk polio vaccine; R. Buckminster Fuller, best known for designing the geodesic dome; and Thomas A. Edison, whose research produced many inventions, including the phonograph and the light bulb.

Ground was broken for the Grace Murray Hopper Service Center of the Navy Regional Data Automation Center in San Diego, California, on September 27, 1985. The facility was named for her in recognition of her extraordinary contributions to the Navy and

Entrance to the Grace Murray Hopper Service Center building, Navy Regional Data Automation Center, San Diego, California.

dedicated at ceremonies held on July 28, 1987. A room at the facility is set aside as a museum to display Grace Hopper's many honorary degrees, awards, and military decorations.

On November 8, 1985, Commodore Grace Murray Hopper's rank was elevated to rear admiral. She became the only woman admiral in the history of the United States Navy. Grace says that when she became a rear admiral, she telephoned her friends in Philadelphia to keep an eye on her great-grandfather Russell's grave because she said, "He may rise from the dead."

Grace Hopper was interviewed on the CBS television program *60 Minutes* on March 6, 1983. Later that same year, on May 27, she was interviewed by the Voice of America. She also was a guest on NBC's David Letterman show on October 2, 1986, an appearance that revealed to the television audience her winsome wit and sense of fun. On January 1, 1987, Grace Hopper was grand marshal of the Orange Bowl Parade. These appearances have highlighted her long and dedicated career.

No matter how many awards Grace Hopper receives, no matter how long she lives, no matter how many more jobs she may have, she still regards the highest award she will ever have as "the privilege and responsibility of serving with true faith and allegiance, very proudly, in the United States Navy." She has given all the honorariums she has received from her speaking engagements to the Navy Relief Society.

Grace Hopper has spent her lifetime trying to change people's minds about many things. She has refused to become complacent about anything to do with the future of computers and the people who will work with those computers. She is a self-made woman who sets a sterling example for young people who want to serve their country.

Dr. Hopper does not believe that young people should waste energy making a life plan. Instead, they should concentrate on preparing themselves to communicate clearly both in speech and in writing, and she says, "grab every opportunity that comes down the pike."

This country's "greatest natural resource" is its young people, Grace Hopper believes. She adds, "We talk about our natural resources, we talk about oil and coal and timber. But our young people are our future. Without them the natural resources will be of no use at all. It's to those young people we must look for the future of this country. And it is to them that we must give the best possible training."

There is something else that Grace Hopper thinks we have forgotten. "Give praise when praise is due. We bawl out people, but how often do we compliment them?"

She recalls a decision she made that every one of her Navy staff had to be able to stand up and give a report and not say "you know."

A cake prepared to celebrate the dedication of the Grace Murray Hopper Service Center at San Diego, California. The cake has one of Admiral Hopper's favorite quotes written on it.

"So, I put a little square box on the desk with a slit in it and if they said 'you know' during the report, they would have to put in a quarter. We didn't take the quarters, but it tied up their capital. You would be surprised at how fast they learned how not to say 'you know.'"

Grace continued, "Then there was a reward. When I was invited to give a presentation for an admiral, I would arrive with my entire crew trailing after me. One by one I would introduce them to give the presentation on their share of the work. I watched those youngsters grow two inches when the admiral said 'well done.'"

Grace Hopper emphasized in her acceptance speech at Brewster Academy, "We must also provide something else for them [young people] that over the last few years we've tended to forget. We thought we could do everything by management. We forgot about leadership. And I mean leadership as I was taught in Midshipman's School, the old-fashioned Navy leadership."

In addition, Dr. Hopper points out, "When the going gets rough, you cannot manage a man into combat; you must lead him. You manage things, you lead people." Today's young people "are looking for positive leadership, the old-fashioned kind, the two-way street, loyalty up and loyalty down," says Grace. She adds, "The most important job [for adults] . . . is to provide that leadership."

Among the many things that Grace Hopper wants to communicate to young people is the necessity to persist and not get frustrated when they have a new idea. She says a really good new idea sometimes takes two to five years to sell to other people. The trick is to quietly keep working on it and not to give up until it works.

Smoking has been a part of Grace Hopper's life since she was twenty-one. She says she started smoking in college, but that people didn't know then that it was dangerous. Her advice to anyone is, "I'd tell them not to start." Further, she counsels, "no smoking, no alcohol, and no drugs." Grace adds, "Never risk anything that will damage your brain. If you are going to enjoy music, pictures, books, anything, you need your mind at its freshest, not damaged by alcohol or drugs. Besides which, the only way you're going to earn a living is using your head."

Grace Hopper also wants young people to know that the people of this country did once all unite and work together toward one goal. During World War II, "Everyone in this country was for one thing," says Grace. And she adds, "I have a sneaking suspicion that if something like Pearl Harbor happened again, the country would turn the same way, totally united."

When asked for her most important achievement, Dr. Hopper replies that her most important work is represented by the hundreds of young students she has taught. She believes education is the key to the future for each of us. Her brother calls her an "inveterate teacher," and her life has borne out her love of teaching.

Grace Hopper's favorite maxim to young people is: "A ship in port is safe, but that is not what ships are built for." She urges each of us to do and dare—to be willing to take risks to accomplish our goals.

There are many shining examples of the continuing legacy of Grace Murray Hopper. One can be seen at our national service academies. Each fall as thousands of raw recruits take their places at Annapolis, West Point, and Colorado Springs, they find personal computers on their desktops. Perhaps they do not fit into a shoebox, but their speed and ease of use would astound Charles Babbage and Ada Byron Lovelace. They fulfill Howard Aiken's dream of a calculating machine. And for Grace Hopper there is the joy of knowing that a large number of America's finest youths have access to computers that can be used as tools to help them attain their hopes and dreams.

One characteristic of Grace Hopper is that she cannot retire. When the Navy retired her at the age of seventy-nine, she went right into a top job in private industry working as a senior consultant for

Digital Equipment Corporation. She is doing what she has enjoyed the most—teaching and getting people interested in computers.

Grace says, "When I get invitations to schools and colleges, I like to go because I like to encourage the youngsters. I like our young people."

And the "youngsters" who have been privileged to hear Grace Hopper speak know that they have been visited by a legendary computer expert, teacher, and American patriot. They are inspired by Grace Hopper and the spirit of her message because she selflessly reaches far beyond the world of computers to touch their lives with her gifts of knowledge and leadership.

Grace Murray Hopper is respectfully and lovingly known as "Amazing Grace, Grandma COBOL, and the Grand Lady of Software." A quotation from a profile of Grace Hopper in the Winter 1982 issue of "Concepts" published by Wang Laboratories sums up by saying, "Through it all, however, she has maintained a warm, soft-spoken manner that doesn't command respect, but carefully wraps it up and carries it away."

What Is COBOL?

COBOL is a highly structured programming language. A COBOL program is always made up of four divisions. They are called Identification, Environment, Data, and Procedure, and they always appear in this order. The Identification Division has no sections, but the Environment and Data divisions are made up of sections, paragraphs, entries, and clauses. The Procedure Division contains sections, paragraphs, sentences, and statements. Each division has a specific job to do within a COBOL program.

The Identification Division gives the COBOL program a name and provides other basic information. The Environment Division describes the type of computers being used to execute the program. The Data division describes the data to be used, and the file section of this division describes the form of the data that will be input to the program or output from the program. The Procedure Division tells the process to be performed.

COBOL has a set of characters that must be used to form COBOL statements. The characters can be numerical, alphabetic, or special, such as a plus sign, minus sign, equal sign, period, or comma. Each character or symbol has a specific use in the COBOL program.

COBOL Character Set

Character	Meaning		
+	plus sign		
-	minus sign or hyphen	arithmetic	
*	asterisk	operators	
/	slash		condition
=	equal sign		tests
>	greater than symbol		
<	less than symbol		
$	currency sign		
.	period		
,	comma		
" or '	quote characters	punctuation	
;	semicolon		
(	left parenthesis		
)	right parenthesis		
0,1,...9	numerical characters (digits)		
A,B,...Z	alphabetic characters (letters)		

Though a COBOL program looks like familiar English, it is a computer language that follows strict rules. Only certain words are recognized as COBOL words. There is a prescribed list of these words that a programmer must adhere to. For example, a programmer could not write the word "transfer" instead of the word "move" in a COBOL program. The computer would not recognize the word "transfer" as a COBOL word.

An example of statements in COBOL follows:

MULTIPLY TOTAL BY 4 GIVING NEW—TOT
MOVE NEW—TOT TO OUTPUT
WRITE OUTPUT

These three statements in COBOL multiply the number in the location called TOTAL by 4. The result is then printed.

A computer language such as COBOL is known as a high-level language. A program written in a high-level language must be translated into machine language before the computer can obey it. A modern computer can do the translation itself.

After writing the program in COBOL, the programmer keys the statements in the program onto punched cards or magnetic tapes or disks. The data or information on the cards, tapes, or disks is a *source program* or the program the programmer writes.

The manufacturer has built into the computer another program known as a *compiler program*. It translates the data in the source program into an *object program* or one the computer understands. The object program is in machine language. Machine language for a modern computer consists of only two digits, zeros and ones.

As you know, computers use a binary system of only two symbols—zero and one–for all of the information that they store or process. All of the characters in the decimal number system and in the alphabet, as well as other symbols, are replaced by a code of zeros and ones.

Another more familiar code that uses only two symbols is Morse code. It replaces the letters of the alphabet and decimal numbers with a code of dots and dashes.

In a computer, the zeros and ones of the binary system are called *bits* (from *bin*ary dig*its*). Eight bits grouped together are a *byte*.

Today, a computer stores information on thousands of molecular-sized bits that are within the microchips of the computer. The bits consist of molecular-sized specks of metal that are either charged with electricity (stands for a 1) or not charged with electricity (stands for a 0).

In the binary system, this string of eight zeros and ones, 10100110, stands for the decimal number 83. Using only zeros and ones may seem like a long and tedious way to write a two digit decimal number, but because computers operate at nearly the speed of light, they can process the strings of zeros and ones faster than the human mind can think.

The zeros and ones of the binary system also can stand for the letters of the alphabet in much the same way that the dots and dashes of Morse Code do.

The importance of COBOL is that it is the most widely used computer business language in the world. COmmon Business Oriented Language is standardized so that it can be used on many different computers and can be understood by users all over the world. In large part, the credit for this extraordinary accomplishment belongs to Dr. Grace Murray Hopper, who led the way from computer codes to COBOL.

Education, Military Record, Awards, and
Professional Activities

EDUCATION

Hartridge School, Plainfield, New Jersey	1924
Vassar College, Poughkeepsie, New York, Bachelor of Arts degree, Phi Beta Kappa	1928
Yale University, New Haven, Connecticut, Master of Arts	1930
Yale University, New Haven, Connecticut, Ph.D., Sigma Xi	1934
Vassar Faculty Fellow, New York University	1941-42

MILITARY RECORD

Apprentice Seaman and Midshipman USNR Midshipman School-W, Northampton, Massachusetts	May 4-June 27, 194.
Lieutenant (junior grade)	June 27, 1944
Lieutenant	June 1, 1946
Lieutenant Commander	April 1, 1952
Commander	July 1, 1957
Retired with rank of Commander	December 31, 1966
Recalled to active duty	August 1, 1967
Captain	August 1, 1973
Commodore	November 8, 1983
Rank of Commodore known as Rear Admiral	November 8, 1985

PROFESSIONAL ACTIVITIES

Instructor to Associate Professor, Department of Mathematics, Vassar College	1931-43
Assistant Professor of Mathematics, Barnard College	1943
Mathematical Officer, United States Navy, Bureau of Ordnance	1944-46
Research Fellow in Engineering Sciences and Applied Physics, Computation Laboratory, Harvard University	1946-49
Senior Mathematician, Eckert-Mauchly Computer Corporation	1949-52
Systems Engineer, Director of Automatic Programming Development, UNIVAC Division of the Sperry Corporation	1952-64
Visiting Lecturer to Adjunct Professor, Moore School of Electrical Engineering, University of Pennsylvania	1959
Staff Scientist, Systems Programming, UNIVAC Division of Sperry Corporation (on military leave 1967-71) retired 1971.	1964-71
Active duty, United States Navy, serving in the Information Systems Division as OP-911F	1967-77

Professorial Lecturer in Management Sciences, George Washington University	1971-78
Active duty, United States Navy, serving as NAVDAC-OOH	1977-86
Senior Consultant, Digital Equipment Corporation	1986-

AWARDS

Phi Beta Kappa	1928
Sigma Xi	1934
Naval Ordnance Development Award	1946
Fellow, Institute of Electrical and Electronics Engineers	1962
Fellow, American Association for the Advancement of Science	1963
Society of Women Engineers, SWE Achievement Award	1964
Institute of Electrical and Electronics Engineers, Philadelphia Section Achievement Award	1968
Connelly Memorial Award, Miami Valley Computer Association	1968
Data Processing Management Association, Computer Science "Man-of-the-Year" Award	1969
Upsilon Pi Epsilon, Honorary Member, Texas A&M, Alpha Chapter	1970
American Mothers Committee, Science Achievement Award	1970
American Federation of Information Processing Societies, Harry Goode Memorial Award	1970
Honorary Doctor of Engineering, Newark College of Engineering, Newark, New Jersey	1972
Wilbur Lucius Cross Medal, Yale University, New Haven, Connecticut	1972
Fellow, Association of Computer Programmers and Analysts	1972
Epsilon Delta Pi, Honorary Member, SUNY Potsdam Chapter, Potsdam, New York	1973
Honorary Doctor of Science, C. W. Post College of Long Island University, Greenvale, New York	1973
Elected to membership in the National Academy of Engineering	1973
Legion of Merit	1973
Distinguished Fellow of the British Computer Society	1973
Honorary Doctor of Laws, University of Pennsylvania, Philadelphia, Pennsylvania	1974
Distinguished Member Award, Washington, D.C. Chapter, Association for Computing Machinery	1976
Honorary Doctor of Science, Pratt Institute	1976

W. Wallace McDowell Award, Institutute of Electrical and Electronic Engineers Computer Society	1976
Honorary Doctor of Science, Linkoping University, Sweden	1980
Honorary Doctor of Science, Bucknell University, Lewisburg, Pennsylvania	1980
Honorary Doctor of Science, Acadia University, Wolfville, Nova Scotia	1980
Navy Meritorious Service Medal	1980
Honorary Doctor of Science, Loyola University, Chicago, Illinois	1981
Honorary Doctor of Science, University of Chicago, Illinois	1981
Honorary Doctor of Science, Southern Illinois University, Carbondale, Illinois	1981
Honorary Doctor of Public Service, George Washington University, Washington, D.C.	1981
Honorary Doctor of Humane Letters, Seton Hill College, Greensburg, Pennsylvania	1982
Honorary Doctor of Science, Marquette University, Milwaukee, Wisconsin	1982
Dedication of the Grace Murray Hopper Center for Computer Learning, Brewster Academy, Wolfeboro, New Hampshire	1983
Honorary Doctor of Business Adminstration, Lake Forest College, Lake Forest, Illinois	1983
Honorary Doctor of Science, Clarkson University, Potsdam, New York	1983
Institute of Electrical and Electronic Engineers Computer Pioneer Medal	1983
Honorary Doctor of Science, Hood College, Frederick, Maryland	1983
Honorary Doctor of Science, Russell Sage College, Troy, New York	1983
Golden Plate Award, American Academy of Achievement, Coronado, California	1983
Honorary Doctor of Science, Villa Julia College, Baltimore, Maryland	1983
American Association of University Women Achievement Award	1983
Federally Employed Women Achievement Award	1983
Association of Computing Machinery Distinguished Service Award	1983
Living Legacy Award, Women's International Center, San Diego, California	1984

Woman of the Year Award, Young Women's Christian
Association of the National Capitol Area   1984
Honorary Doctor of Science, University of Maryland,
College Park, Maryland   1984
Honorary Doctor of Laws, Smith College, Northampton,
Massachusetts   1984
Honorary Doctor of Science, St. Peter's College, Jersey
City, New Jersey   1984
Honorary Doctor of Science, Worcester State College,
Worcester, Massachusetts   1984
Honorary Doctor of Science, Hartwick College, Oneonta,
New York   1984
Honorary Doctor of Business Administration, Providence
College, Providence, Rhode Island   1984
Honorary Doctor of Science, City College of Morris,
Morristown, New Jersey   1984
Honorary Doctor of Science, Bloomsburg College,
Bloomsburg, Pennsylvania   1984
Honorary Doctor of Science, Aurora College, Aurora, Ohio   1985
Honorary Doctor of Science, Wright State University,
Dayton, Ohio   1985
Honorary Doctor of Letters, Western New England
College, Spring field, Massachusetts   1985
Honorary Doctor of Laws, College of William and Mary,
Williams burg, Virginia   1985
Honorary Doctor of Science, Rivier College, Nashua,
New Hampshire   1985
Honorary Doctor of Science, Marist College, Pough-
keepsie, New York   1985
Honorary Doctor of Science, Saint John Fisher College,
Rochester, New York   1985
Honorary Doctor of Science, Syracuse University,
Syracuse, New York   1986
Honorary Doctor of Humane Letters, Caldwell College,
Caldwell, New Jersey   1986
Honorary Doctor of Science, University of Massachusetts
at Amherst, Amherst, Massachusetts   1986
Honorary Doctor of Military Science, Northeastern
University, Boston, Massachusetts   1986
Honorary Doctor of Letters, Drexel University, Drexel,
Pennsylvania   1987

OTHER AWARDS

Fellow of the Institute for the Certification of Computer Professionals	1981
Gold Medal, Armed Forces Communications and Electronics Association	1982
Ada August Lovelace Award, Association of Women in Computing	1983
Beta Phi Sigma, George Washington University Chapter, Washington, D.C.	1984
Jane Addams Award, Rockford College, Rockford, Illinois	1984
Andrus Award, American Association of Retired Persons Annual Award	1984
Institute of Electrical and Electronics Engineers Centennial Award	1984
Engineering and Science Hall of Fame, Dayton, Ohio	1984
U.S.S. *Constitution* Museum, Samuel Eliot Morison Award for Distinguished Service, Boston, Massachusetts	1984
INFOMART Information Processing Hall of Fame, Dallas, Texas	1985
Award of Merit, American Consulting Engineer Council, Colorado Springs, Colorado	1985
Honorary Navy Recruiters, United States Navy Recruiting Command	1985
Henry T. Heald Award, Illinois Institute of Technology, Chicago, Illinois	1985
Lifetime Achievement Award, Federation of Government Information Processing Councils	1986
Unsung Heroine Award, Ladies Auxiliary to the Veterans of Foreign Wars	1986
Distinguished Achievement Award, American Aging Association	1986
Meritorious Citation, Navy Relief Society	1986
Navy Distinguished Service Medal	1986
The Charles Holmes Pette Medal, University of New Hampshire, Durham, New Hampshire	1988
The Emanuel R. Piore Award, Institute of Electrical and Electronics Engineers	1988

Further Reading

Gilbert, Lynn, and Moore, Gaylen. *Particular Passions,* Clarkson, New York: N. Potter, Inc. 1981, pp. 58-63.

Green, Laura. *Computer Pioneers,* New York: Franklin Watts, 1985, pp.77-80.

Hyde, Margaret O. *Artificial Intelligence,* Hillside, New Jersey: Enslow Publishers, 1986.

Mandrell, S. and Hopper, G.M. *Understanding Computers,* St. Paul: West Publishing, 1984.

Mompoullan, Chantal. *Voices of America: Interviews with Eight American Women of Achievement,* Washington, D.C.: U.S. Information Agency, 1984.

Science Year, 1987. Chicago: World Book Inc., 1986, pp. 337-357.

Slater, Robert. *Portraits in Silicon,* Cambridge, MA: Massachusetts Institute of Technology, 1987, Chapter 20, "Bugs, Compilers, and COBOL."

Wetzstein, Cheryl, and Forristal, Linda Joyce. *The World and I,* August, 1987, "Grace Murray Hopper," pp. 198-205.

Zientara, Marguerite. *The History of Computing,* CW Communications, Inc., 1981, Part 11, "Captain Grace M. Hopper and the Genesis of Programming Languages," pp. 51-53.

INDEX